The Third Step of the Stairs

The
Third Step
of the
Stairs

Christine Hall

Matador
Unit E2 Airfield Business Park,
Harrison Road, Market Harborough,
Leicestershire. LE16 7UL
Tel: 0116 2792299
Email: books@troubador.co.uk
Web: www.troubador.co.uk/matador
Twitter: @matadorbooks

ISBN 978 1803135 342

British Library Cataloguing in Publication Data.
A catalogue record for this book is available from the British Library.

Printed and bound in Great Britain by CMP UK
Typeset in 11pt Adobe Caslon Pro by Troubador Publishing Ltd, Leicester, UK

Matador is an imprint of Troubador Publishing Ltd

To Jim, a loving, patient and devoted Husband,
Father, Grandfather and Great Grandfather.

To my children and family who are my everything.

PROLOGUE

The stairs at the house where I was born and raised became a familiar place to sit and hide, it ran through the middle with a door which closed it off from the lounge.

Coats were hung on the back of the door giving me something else to hide under.

The carpet was a faded dark green, threadbare and held in place with brass grippers dulled with age.

The walls were painted in plain eggshell emulsion stippled so that little clumps solidified in tiny peaks like icing on a Christmas cake, picking them off gave me something to do to while away what seemed like hours, waiting for the door to open and Dad to return from the pub worse the wear from drink.

At the foot of the stairs was a shoe rack being one of six children meant there were a lot of shoes, sorting them into pairs while hiding filled some time too.

The third step was just the right height to sit on and still keep my feet firmly planted on the floor in case I had to jump up quickly to either escape to the bedroom or charge into the lounge to try to protect mum from a beating.

My mouth was dry, my stomach seemed to be tied in a knot, I breathed quietly listening intently for his approaching footsteps.

This situation wasn't unique just to me it was experienced by my four sisters and my brother. I was the second eldest and felt like I had to protect everyone.

The younger siblings especially were terrified when arguments and fights started and would take a lot of consoling.

My life began in March 1941, a wartime conception, a difficult breech birth so my mother always told me, maybe this was the reason I had a bigger sized rear than my siblings.

The house was a middle one in a terrace of four with a shared entry and a pathway which went round the back of the houses.

There were three bedrooms, after we had all arrived the five girls shared one room, one set of bunks and three sharing a double bed, my brother having the tiny box room to himself.

There was no toilet or bathroom upstairs so chamber pots were used, although in the girls' room we did have the luxury of a wash stand a basin and a big jug to hold the cold water to wash in.

The ground floor consisted of a kitchen with a large Belson sink, a wooden draining board, underneath was a bath with cold running water only.

On top of the bath was a wooden lid which served as a worktop but had to be lifted off on bath nights.

In the corner of the kitchen stood a copper which was filled with water, and a coal fire was lit underneath providing hot water for bathing and for washdays.

Bath nights were usually on a Friday night, the same water being used by all of us topped up with a bucket of hot water as required, I still recall the gritty sensation at the bottom of the bath.

Hair washing was also done on this night plus the weekly ritual of the Derbac comb followed by the ceremony of the curl rags, mum tied them into our wet hair pulling the scalp so tightly we almost looked Chinese, sleeping in them was persecution like placing your head on a bed of rocks but the results the next day were lovely ringlets which friends were jealous of.

The middle room was the lounge heated with a coal fire in a large cooking range, the heavy metal oven shelves on cold nights were wrapped in a blanket and put into our beds, if you were the last to go to bed you were unfortunate to have the shelf which was knobbly.

Getting the fire to start was quite a task, first the kindling, then scrunched up paper, then the coal, light with a match, hold in front of the fireplace with your forehead and outstretched arms a larger sheet of newspaper to attempt to draw the fire to burn, always this ended with paper catching light and having to bundle it up into the fireplace to prevent a house fire.

A small passage under the stairs led between the lounge and the front room here was a walk in cupboard called the glory hole it was always stuffed to the brim so was difficult to walk in but we found a space to escape when playing hide and seek.

There were cases of clothes Mum kept to alter to fit us, pots of paint, Dads bits of engineering stuff, toys, empty cases although holidays were a non – event, hanging on the inside of the door were gas masks we'd have fun scaring each other wearing these.

The front room was used on Sundays, high days and special days we'd light a fire in here by carrying a shovel full of hot coals through from the lounge often coals would fall off and you could smell the rug singeing.

As we got older and had boyfriends the first to get home and light the fire made claim to the room for the evening , much to the annoyance of the ones who missed out.

The floor covering in all the rooms was lino with handmade peg rugs laid over the top we took turns sharing jobs around the house, whoever was cleaning had to lift the rugs take them outside and give them a good beating, they were so heavy and held on to a lot of grit.

Mum had strong Christian values having been raised in a strict Methodist household but this was not shared by Dad and would often be the cause of conflict and arguments between them, however we did all go to Sunday school.

Each year there was a Sunday school anniversary, this was always exciting as mum who was a trained seamstress made us new dresses, she would source her materials from old curtains, by unpicking old clothes or buying on credit.

We did have new shoes for this occasion and I can still smell the leather and hear the sound my new shoes made on the pavement as we walked to Chapel.

Mum also took in orders for dressmaking and alterations which brought a bit of extra revenue in to help with the housekeeping as Dad didn't give her a lot of money.

Dad was an accomplished pianist I was told he was a professionally trained singer, he did have a lovely tenor voice and was often in demand for his talents, he sang in a Police male voice choir, had leading roles in local Gilbert and Sullivan and musical society productions. He also was out a lot entertaining in pubs and clubs.

It was hearing him sing when I admired him most and maybe have him to thank for introducing me to music and singing and my love of the theatre, but unfortunately other aspects of his life and behaviour showed him in a different light.

ONE

EARLY YEARS

Growing up in our house at times was difficult, dysfunctional, and violent, it was busy too with children coming along at almost two yearly intervals but somehow we plodded along accepting that this was the norm, a way of life we got used to.

There was no bus service so we'd walk about two miles to school, an old lady who lived opposite the school had a tuck shop and sold windfall apples we were allowed to buy several items for a penny she was always generous and gave us lots more.

School dinners were quite a treat apart from the watery cabbage which I hated; the smell of it cooking still lingers today when I talk about it.

I enjoyed most lessons apart from P E wearing just knickers and vest I was self– conscious and always felt the teacher was ogling me.

Our own fun was created building dens, climbing trees, playing on the railway banks, putting out fires which had started when the sparks from the steam trains set the banks alight.

We made imitation guns with sticks and cocoa tin lids, imagined we were soldiers escaping from the Germans, hiding under bridges behind bushes and in the railway tunnel.

We ran through the tunnels behind the trains and got covered in soot and smoke which we foolishly thought could be washed off with water from a nearby spring this water was so clear cold and refreshing when we were thirsty.

Dad found out and I remember getting the buckle end of his belt when I returned home, I refused to cry and didn't show that it hurt.

Roller skating was my favourite hobby the skates were the best present I ever had, I had to carry a spanner with me at all times as the bolts were always coming loose.

Never academically bright I failed my eleven plus exams so I was sent to a secondary modern girl's school at Stockingford near Nuneaton.

I don't know why I was sent to an all girls' school perhaps it was because most of my friends were boys and the oldies were trying to tell me something.

As it happened it didn't matter as the boy's school was right next door and we met up on the playing field anyway.

At this school I found most of the lessons tedious except for music and drama Mrs Bennett was the teacher, she was full of enthusiasm and had a beautiful singing voice which matched her looks.

Always neat and trim her clothes fashionable, I longed to mimic her style, her hair was black and wavy her piercing green eyes looked directly at you when she gave instruction, I vowed I would one day wear bright red lipstick and be like her.

Passionate about her music, singing and drama she was a true inspiration.

I did throw the discus for the team and wore proper sportswear thankfully.

*

A fair came and set up in the field next to our row of houses it was so exciting, watching it being put together, we could hear the music the noise of the rides and the bumper cars banging.

The sounds of laughter and screams of joy echoed in the air and the sweet smell of candy floss and toffee apples penetrated the nose.

I never wanted it to end and decided I would run away with them when they left, besides there was a good looking traveller I fell in love with, I woke up in the morning to find I'd missed the opportunity as they had gone in the night.

Grocery shopping was done on my bike, riding across three fields and lifting the bike over two stiles to get to the Co-op at Ansley Hall so Mum could claim her dividend, her number 1971 is imprinted on my brain.

With three or four large bags I set off on the return journey balancing eggs in a brown paper bag, no such things as egg boxes then. When reaching the stile the bags were lifted over first followed by the bike which was then reloaded, then me, it was quite precarious cycling back across the furrows of the field without falling off, breaking jars or smashing the eggs.

My reward was a tin of Horlicks tablets, little compressed squares of solid Horlicks in a tin.

On Saturday we would catch the bus to go shopping for fresh fruit and vegetables at Nuneaton market, the smell of a stick of celery and red apples still lingers.

If there was any money to spare mum treated us to a chip and mushy pea lunch with a slice of bread and butter at the fish restaurant. It was a real luxury.

Occasional Saturday mornings we were allowed pocket money to go to the ABC Minors at the Ritz cinema in Nuneaton where we watched Lassie, Dan Dare, Popeye and Mickey Mouse films. And sing songs.

*

School holidays were a non– event at our house, no trips to the seaside were ever arranged apart from an occasional day trip with the Sunday school or the local pub, we did have a short trip to Blackpool when Dad won some money from gambling either on horses or football, this was the reason we were short of money.

He borrowed a car from my uncle who had his own taxi business, there were five children at this point so we all piled into the car and headed off to Blackpool.

Staying near the fun fair was great although he didn't give us any pocket money for rides I clearly recall us standing laughing hysterically at the gyrating mechanical clown encased in a glass cabinet at the fairground entrance.

Watching other children on the rides while we didn't have money to go on, was sad but it was still special being there in the atmosphere.

Playing on the sands was fun burying each other, there was sand in everything, keeping an eye on the younger ones was a task, we managed to lose Rosemary the youngest.

The car had been parked at the top of a multi storey car park, when we returned to commence the homeward journey and were safely in, it wouldn't start Dad shouted, "Christine get out and push," so I did.

It started he revved it up and off he went leaving me racing behind all the way to the bottom I was terrified they would go without me.

The remainder of the Summer holidays was spent in the fields or at the brook, come rain or shine we'd make sandwiches, fat slices of crusty bread spread thickly with jam, no butter.

Rhubarb sticks with a little newspaper bag of sugar, and a bottle of water made up our picnic and off we'd go.

Mother had made us bathing suits, not very glamorous, stitched all through with shearing elastic so that one size fitted all, they seemed to grow with us, especially when wet, at least she knew that all her girls were well covered.

Mum trusted us older ones to be responsible for the younger ones to make sure they came to no harm.

We walked about a mile across fields to the brook climbing trees and playing hide and seek on the way, the brook had a shallow end with a bridge over, here the water ran quickly washing the shale and pebbles we could see sticklebacks and water boatmen.

The deeper end was our favourite spot it had a sludgy sandy bottom so didn't hurt our feet, dragon flies flitted around, the sunlight flickering on their wings.

A rope swing suspended from a tree hung over the water it gave us hours of fun, we'd climb the tree, sit on the big knot at the bottom of the rope, swing high and on the way down let go screaming loudly, landing a belly flop into the water wetting anyone picnicking on the bank.

Feeling hungry and exhausted we sat in a circle in the field sharing the sandwiches it felt like a banquet Mum's home– made Strawberry jam was sweet delicious and fruity. The rhubarb was sharp even though it was dipped in sugar, it made your teeth feel furry.

The bottle of water was passed around and we all had a slurp, I didn't know water could taste so good.

Drying ourselves on the one towel mum had allowed us we headed for home, it always seemed to take longer to get home, with the younger ones demanding to be carried or piggy backed.

It was good to arrive home, mum worrying if we were alright and about to send a search party, we had no idea how long we had been out.

After a hot bath hair washing and a comforting supper it was time for bed.

*

At junior school there was great excitement when I was chosen to play Mrs Bagwash the wicked stepmother in a production of Cinderella, my younger sister Sonia played the lead role, my cousin Frank played Buttons.

I must have been ten or eleven, it was such fun I felt very important, during the dress rehearsal I recall tripping and falling over, the costume I wore had a bustle which bounced in the air causing quite a laugh, the teacher said do that every night so I did and added more comedy with each show.

And so my love for drama and acting began it is something to escape to and which has fulfilled me during my life.

At home we had a wind up gramophone which was regularly used for dance sessions in the front room. Jiving was our speciality we competed with each other especially my brother Duncan who was very good.

Pearl my eldest sister acquired a taste for classical music and had a long playing record of Swan Lake, during a jive session I hadn't noticed that she had left it on the settee I fell and landed on it shattering it, I think she's only just forgiven me.

She did get her own back later, for my fifteenth birthday I was given a beautiful white duffle coat with red toggles and a red tartan lining, I felt really special in it, one day I couldn't find it, it was missing for weeks and no one admitting to taking it.

When I was tidying the glory hole the cupboard under the stairs I found it with black oil on it, which by then had penetrated too much to clean off.

Pearl had borrowed it gone out on a motorbike ride with one of her boyfriends, draped it over the engine and did the damage. Her red face when she confessed gave her away.

I think I have forgiven her now.

One November the fifth I dressed Sonia up as Guy Fawkes and pushed her from house to house in an old pushchair asking " Penny for the Guy", I was doing quite well until Billy Greenway the village bully came up and punched her in the stomach shouting "that's no guy" she leapt out and ran all the way home, leaving me chasing furiously behind with an empty pushchair.

Sonia was accident prone one day climbing the metal railings to get to the railway she stuck a spike in her hand, another day while playing on a hay rick she slipped and broke her arm.

I piggy backed her home with her arm hanging and swinging limply and crying loudly, Passing my Grandmas house I spotted dad up a ladder painting, he saw us and shouted "what's the matter Christine" I replied " Sonia's broken her arm". He just carried on painting.

*

We had close family friends known as Uncle Alf and Aunty Lilian who owned a large farm at the bottom of the village, we spent many happy times there especially when the fruit ripened in the orchard we picked them, wrapped them and stored them in their loft.

In October there was a school holiday called the potato picking holiday, uncle Alf fetched us from the village on his open trailer and we'd bounce all the way to the farm screeching with laughter.

A machine turned the soil over, and on our knees, we picked the spuds and filled sacks it, was back aching but the reward was wonderful, Aunty came walking across the field with a basket full of cheese and onion rolls fresh apples and flasks of tea, it tasted so good.

We were also allowed to fill a sack to take home, mum was thrilled and we picked the biggest we could find to have as jacket potatoes.

The hay field at the back of our house was cut each year by machine and then with pitch forks we'd help load it up on the wagon, the farmer always left a triangle of uncut hay in the middle of the field to trap the rabbits so that he could shoot them and sell them usually he gave mum one, she showed me how to skin it. It was very tasty cooked in a stew, not much was wasted.

I was desperate for a bike, dad had an old rusting bike frame in the garden, it had no tyres, inner tubes or saddle, but I got it out and took it into the street. I managed to ride it up and down the road although it was rusty and creaked.

I bounced it over the kerb and the pipe which the saddle should fit on stuck into my buttock I made such a noise the neighbours came rushing out to check on me and helped me home.

I remember how embarrassed I was exposing my backside to everyone and Pearl shrieking" Ooh mum there's jelly coming out."

Needless to say I did have to visit the doctor for stitches.

TWO

THE CORNER SHOP

The doorway of the corner shop provided us village youngsters with a haven to play in, hide in, court in and shelter in, but only after the shop was closed.

The shop was owned by Alice an elderly spinster who terrified me, she reminded me of a witch with straggly black hair, piercing eyes and yellow skin.

She always had a cigarette hanging out of her mouth, I would stare waiting for the long ash to drop off and wondered if it would land in the food.

The shop inside was like a cave of wonder, on the counter was a rare mixture of cakes, bread, fruit, stale vegetables, sticks of kindling, and a large set of weighing scales.

I remember a long thin bladed knife she used to carve the ham and bacon with, her finger nails were long, dirty and stained with nicotine, she never did wash her hands before doing this.

A side of bacon which was never covered up except for the netting clinging to it, hung in front of the shelves.

On the floor around the shop were sacks containing flour, oats, coal, slack and sugar these items were all loose so had to be weighed and put into brown paper bags.

The shelves sagged under the weight of the tins and boxes containing different foods.

Alice also sold paraffin, she filled up bottles for the customers using a metal jug and a funnel, the smell hung in the air and I am sure flavoured the food.

The bay windows were full of glass jars containing every imaginable sweet, lemon bon-bons, Pontefract cakes, liquorish sticks and liquorish wood, barley sugar, mint humbugs they were a real temptation.

In the front of the window the boxes and packets had faded and spilled their contents which had rolled out mingling with the dead flies and dust and dirt, they must have been there for years. I thought what a waste as sweets for us were a rarity.

Occasionally I was given some pocket money and with the ration book I brought my favourite, flying saucers which were made from rice paper and melted in your mouth with an explosion of sherbet inside.

One day a "for sale" sign went up outside the shop and we learned that Alice had had a stroke and could no longer manage; she didn't have any relatives to take over so the corner shop had to close.

I felt guilty that my thoughts and feelings about Alice had been so bad after all she had never harmed me she was just a unique sort of person providing a service to the village in a way only she knew how.

What a loss it was to lose something that was such an institution and benefit, even I and my friends felt the loss.

Eventually poor Alice's shop was knocked down to make way for new houses and she became just a memory, I suppose it's called progress.

*

A memory which stuck in my mind for years was when I was playing out in the street as it was getting dusk, when bats swooped across the entry, Pearl my eldest sister was sent to call me in, she shouted "Christine you've got to come in now, if you don't the bats will stick in your hair and suck your blood"

I crawled as flat on my stomach as I could over the rough gravelled path along the entry grazing my skin and trembling in fear until I got into the house.

I still have a phobia about bats.

There was one time I asked if I could learn to play the trumpet but I wasn't allowed, instead Dad said I could join the Arley Welfare choir which was run by the band and choir master from the next village, Dad also sang with the choir. This was a mining village where more activities took place than in our own village of Ansley. It was great singing with the band, entering competitions, visiting other towns and putting on concerts.

One concert was held at Leamington Spa, a lovely town with a river, we had time to spare before the concert so one of the lads from the band who I had been smitten with invited me to go for a boat ride. It was quite romantic, him doing the rowing, me reclining, dangling my hands in the water until I pulled one out and it was draped in a condom, I felt very embarrassed I think I was only sixteen.

Dances were held every week at the Arley Miners Welfare Hall, I loved dancing and was always desperate to go, and money was an issue as I couldn't afford the bus fare and the admission charge.

The hall was two miles away so the only option was to walk. It was a lonely route, no houses and hedges on both sides of the path, in daylight it was fine but after dark quite scary. I walked in the middle of the road singing "Onward Christian Soldiers" very loudly thinking it would protect me, I was relieved to get home.

Another influence on my life was our neighbours Mr and Mrs Montgomery who had no children so they made a fuss of us. I spent many hours round there house where she would involve me and teach me many things.

A favourite was making peg rugs, cutting strips of material up from old clothes then with a little gadget pull them through a large piece of sacking creating patterns with the different colours and textures.

She did lots of preserving as did mum, so chopping vegetables for piccalilli and chutneys became a regular pastime , she tried to show me how to knit and crochet but I didn't have the patience to sit as they didn't grow fast enough.

Mrs M did lots of baking pastries and cakes, I watched as she mixed the pastry, she was a big lady, I was fascinated to see the fat at the top of her arms wobble backwards and forwards as she rubbed the lard into the flour, I just hoped mine never looked like that.

THREE

CHRISTMAS

We knew Christmas was on the way when mum began all of her preparations, it was a memorable time for many reasons, Dad while he didn't engage much with us did go across the fields prior to Christmas to cut a Holly tree from the hedgerow, I don't know if it was legal but we were happy to have a tree.

Decorating it was tough getting prickled and scratched putting the trimmings on, each year the fairy for the top came out, she had eyes which blinked, pearly teeth and her hair was made from real hair a bit like a wig.

The old blown glass ornaments were carefully unwrapped and we had real dainty candles which clipped on like a peg and lit with a match, I don't know how safe these were but they looked lovely.

Mum made Christmas puddings in a pansion, we all had a stir and made a wish she even poured milk stout into it which smelled strong. The mixture was put into basins covered in greaseproof paper and pudding cloths and then steamed for several hours in the kitchen copper. Christmas day before serving it she hid sixpences and silver charms in it.

Her Christmas cake was divine with lots of marzipan and frosted icing like a snow scene and the old decorations on top, a snowman, robin an elf on a sledge and a Father Christmas carrying a tree.

Christmas Eve I plucked and drew two chickens we had these most years, I bent over the bath in the kitchen and dropped the feathers in, sometimes I had to use pliers to remove the tail and wing feathers as they were too tough to pull by hand.

I cut the feet off and stretched the sinews so that once they were removed I could pull them and make the toes move up and down and make the other children scream.

Drawing the chickens was fun, getting my hands inside, removing its innards, bowel gizzard, heart and liver making sure nothing was left behind, most of this was boiled to make a rich stock for the gravy.

The only time I can remember making my Dad laugh was when I came out of the pantry dancing with a naked chicken.

There was a large cupboard in mums bedroom where she hid the presents, we used to hunt for them, the smells coming out of the cupboard gave things away, there were usually tangerines, bright red apples, nuts, figs and dates, pillow cases and socks were hung on the bedposts the excitement on Christmas Eve was tangible.

Christmas morning started early, Mum had filled socks with an apple, tangerine, nuts and tiny items like pencil sharpeners, marbles, pencils and a rubber, we'd sit on the beds, eyes closed, feeling the shapes to guess what was inside.

One year we put some string across between two beds to try to trip Santa up so that we could catch him in action, but Mum came into the room early and removed it.

How mum managed to buy gifts and do what she did I don't know but we always had plenty, she must have taken in lots of extra sewing and squirrelled the money away.

Dad would still go off to the pub and come back drunk so our joy and euphoria was short lived, it just became a way of life sitting on the third step and waiting.

Dads approaching footsteps when he had been to the pub always made me feel sick, my stomach felt as if it was churning I clenched my teeth and gripped my hands until my nails dug in.

One Saturday lunch time he returned, his dinner was either plated or waiting in saucepans to be cooked, angry or dissatisfied he would open the lounge window and fling the pans through into the garden or throw the plate at the wall, there was little pleasing him.

Late at night he'd return and start goading or hitting Mum, that's when I charged in to break them up and intervene physically stopping him attacking her.

One day I tried to stop him I leaped on his back to pull him away and got hit in the face resulting in a nosebleed, crying and holding my nose I dashed down the road to fetch the police and the doctor.

Mrs Martin a neighbour saw me and said, "What's wrong Christine" I shouted "My Dads gone bloody mad and I'm getting the police and doctor to help". Needless to say neither they nor the neighbours were interested in helping.

There was one day when he chased Mum up the garden and she cut her leg badly on a cloche, the doctor did come then as she needed stiches.

I think most of the village knew of his reputation, as a singer and pianist he was always dressed immaculately, clean shirt, smart, nails filed but no one ever saw the other side of him, although immediate neighbours knew because they would hear the rows through the walls.

Even his own siblings who all lived in the village denied or dismissed his behaviour when they were told.

An incident still so vivid I can't erase it from my mind is when Mum came into our bedroom to sleep and locked the door.

Dad drunk again came upstairs shouting and banging demanding she came out, we sat huddled together terrified, wondering what was going to happen, the younger ones crying and shaking, us older ones trying to keep them quiet and shushing them.

The lock on the door eventually broke and he dragged Mum to their bedroom, we could hear the noises coming from the room but we felt too numb to do anything.

What ensued must have been terrible for Mum I suppose as she had objected and tried to resist it was tantamount to rape and at that time was a husbands' right.

While our early childhood days were a mixture of joy, sadness, confusion, dysfunction and pain we all managed to grow and thrive in a fairly normal way although we must all carry some scars and emotions which erupt from time to time.

FOUR

TEENAGE YEARS

I left school at fifteen not really knowing for sure what I wanted to do, I thought I'd like to go into farming as I loved spending time at my 'Uncle and Aunties" farm and especially loved the animals.

I changed my mind one day while delivering papers on my paper round, getting stuck in a snowdrift and thinking to myself this isn't for me being out in the fields in all weathers so decided to become a nurse.

I was accepted to commence training as a Nursing cadet, the interview was held at Nuns Croft in Nuneaton, a sombre building behind huge trees, previously a residence for Nuns who belonged to St Marys' Abbey nearby.

With a dry mouth and knots in my stomach I recall climbing the big stone steps and ringing the bell, the door opened slowly by a little elderly lady, "Hello I'm Christine Perry I have an appointment" "Come on in follow me" she said and led me into the entrance hall.

It was long and narrow light shone in from a stained glass window reflecting colours onto the patterned Victorian tiles on the floor " Are you here for the interviews" she asked, I confirmed that I was and she took me to wait in a room with desks and chairs.

I discovered later she was the housekeeper.

This was the training school for the two hospitals, The George Eliot and the Manor Hospital; the nurses came here for their lectures and practical training.

I learned that two and a half days a week would be spent at the technical college studying, maths, English, spoken English, history of nursing, and other things, the remainder of the week to be spent at the hospital in the wards and departments. This would continue for three years until I was eighteen and would then start my general training to become a State Registered Nurse.

My first placement was at Nuns Croft where the housekeeper who was a real gem took me under her wings, I cleaned, polished made tea for the Sister tutors and the nurses, tea was always served with arrowroot biscuits.

Cleaning the specimen cupboards was a favourite task I was fascinated by the jars and their contents, appendix, cysts, tumours, tapeworms, foetus at various stages of development, they were all preserved in formaldehyde which occasionally leaked, the smell stung your eyes and nose and took your breath, even so I spent longer on this task than I should have.

The housekeeper who walked with a stoop had beautiful skin reminded me of my grandmother, she introduced me to camomile tea saying that was the recipe for her good skin and long life, she was in her seventies and was amazing, she made it for me to try so I was compelled to drink it even though I hated the taste.

The departments I worked in were Physiotherapy, Path lab, Out Patients, Part Three which was the work house and still had residents, and Pharmacy.

In Physio I switched the wax baths on so they were melted when patients arrived, and had fun testing the wax on my hands then peeling it off again, it was warm and comforting dipping my hands in and building up the layers. I could see how beneficial this treatment would be for patients with arthritis, trauma, or neurological problems.

I made sure the trolley beds were made, the heat lamps switched on and generally helped and observed.

In Path lab it was fascinating looking at specimens, bacteria growing on jelly in petri dishes, testing urine specimens, using a centrifuge, counting the number of abnormal cells on blood specimens under the microscope, I loved this department.

Peter the head technician was dishy too he was rugged, sturdily built, had freckles was down to earth and had a sense of humour but was also patient and encouraging. The whole experience impressed me.

Pharmacy was interesting learning about drugs, filling bottles with lotions and medicines, counting tablets, labelling bottles and jars, scooping leeches and putting them into jars for staff to take to the ward, washing bottles and removing labels.

Out patients enabled me to have more direct contact with patients although the Sister in charge was a bit of a bully, one day the clean laundry arrived, it was my job to tidy the cupboard and put the clean away.

There were cockroaches in between the sheets, I screamed and said," I can't touch these Sister" I hated anything that crawled but in front of the patients she shouted "don't be ridiculous nurse they won't bite "and forced me to do it, I had nightmares for days.

Part Three or the Workhouse as it was known still had residents although it was old and Dickensian the residents felt safe and secure. It was a rather sombre place, dark and fusty smelling.

It was made worse by the Matron in charge of the workhouse, she always had a lit cigarette hanging out of her mouth coughing and spluttering, blowing ash everywhere, she was a large lady with a bladder weakness so when she coughed she leaked her knickers were often seen drying on the radiators.

Being a Nursing cadet was a brilliant introduction to nursing and gave a sound foundation to my future career, highlighting the fact that the patient being at the centre was the crucial factor in becoming a nurse, It familiarised me with hospital life, personnel, buildings, procedures, activities, respect and discipline.

FIVE

VILLAGE LIFE AND ACTIVITIES

I joined several groups in the village as there was little else happening, I did belong to the Brownies when I was younger but out grew them and moved on to the Guides which I didn't enjoy very much. The annual parade to the cenotaph was the only thing I did enjoy, being on parade in uniform and marching through the village with other groups following a band made me tingle inside.

At seventeen I enrolled with the Young Farmers, this was great fun, mixed company, doing robust things like visiting farms, hoe downs in barns, haymaking, cookery lessons, tractor driving and rallies, this was all much more stimulating and exciting, especially getting to know John Townshend a handsome young farmer.

It occurred to my friends and I that a dance in the area was needed for all age groups to attend so went ahead and planned one, we hired a room at Ansley Hall Colliery, made and sold tickets, collected records together, two lads were taking charge of the music. We already had a record player.

We got parents on side who contributed sandwiches and cakes, the local pub gave us pop on a sale and return basis and as the hall was only a mile away everyone managed to walk there.

The excitement was unimaginable, the fact that we had done it all ourselves made us feel very proud, even the Nuneaton Observer came and took a picture.

After the success of the dance I and my two best friends Carol Bates and Ruby Webb began running whist drives which were held once a month in the chapel schoolroom, we begged prizes from local shops and would buy some when we had made enough money from the entrance fees, these too were successful and were well supported.

As I attended Chapel I started to run a Sunday school youth club which ran every week in the schoolroom so there was no hire charge, the Congregational Church funded equipment like skipping ropes, a medicine ball, table tennis , board games and playing cards. We served teas and juice.

We were overseen by some of the church elders but mostly they left us to it, we did open the youth club up to village children who didn't attend chapel too so had quite a number attending.

Sadly I had to give this up once I had started my nurse training because of the shift patterns and requests for a regular evening off was unheard of, however it continued to run and I felt I had achieved something worthwhile.

*

A new housing estate was built to accommodate mine workers from Durham, Scotland and Newcastle to come and work in the local collieries, this created a major change for the village and for the locals. The village which previously was just one long main street with houses on both sides, two small shops and a chip shop now expanded across three fields taking a big chunk of the countryside.

We kids didn't mind it meant we'd have new friends it was quite exciting when they began to move in, even more fun when they started school, at first it was as if they spoke in a foreign language as their accents were so strong especially the Scottish ones. However they were quite normal and we made friends quickly.

New Year's Eve celebrations were amazing, these newcomers opened their houses up to anyone and we went from one house to another sharing celebration, food and drink. I had never seen so much food, pastries, cakes of every description, hot meats and soups, this sort of thing never happened before in our village.

I made a special friend, a good looking boy called George Parks he had gorgeous brown eyes, beautiful teeth and smile and dark wavy hair, I really thought I was in love and would hang around near his house just waiting to catch him. He made me feel weak at the knees and a bit tongue tied.

I spent ages prior to meeting him to make myself look special, I used calamine lotion as a foundation on my face as I couldn't afford much make up but did have mascara with a little brush which I spat in to moisten and shared my sisters' lipstick to use as rouge as well as using on my lips.

Things seemed to be going well until early one evening I followed him across the allotments, he was with my younger sister Sonia. I screamed a few obscenities at her threatened to punch her and went home in tears, I thought it was too good to last and was heartbroken for weeks

At the regular weekly dance, feeling a bit like a gooseberry and not very interested, another boy asked me to dance he was tall fair haired also had nice teeth, so I accepted, he was a good dancer and could jive well, I learned he had his own barbers shop and his parents owned the fish and chip shop in Gun Hill, the next village where we would often go for a bag of chips and to help dig the eyes out of the potatoes.

His mum and Dad were lovely people and I know they thought a lot of me so felt I had to try to make our relationship work. Peter and I met up and went out together for some time but there wasn't a real spark and we gradually drifted apart, which left me feeling guilty.

I decided I'd give up on boyfriends and concentrate on my future and career, my nursing cadet course was coming to an end and I had been accepted to start my general nurse training to become a State Registered Nurse.

SIX

STATE REGISTERED NURSE TRAINING

The first day as new recruits we were met by Miss Clamp, the home sister who had responsibility for us as student nurses.

She issued us with uniforms, purple striped dresses with a plain purple belt and frilly cuffs. I couldn't wait to try it on it looked and felt so different from the harsh scratchy pink overall I wore as a nursing cadet.

She then handed me a stiff rectangular piece of material which apparently was a hat. I had admired the butterfly caps worn by the student nurses and couldn't imagine how I could possibly turn this item into a cap.

Home Sister demonstrated how to fold the material into a concertina, turn it in half, secure with a paper clip and spread the fan shape into a butterfly; she made it look so easy.

After five or six attempts I succeeded ending up with a slightly wilted butterfly.

I met the group of girls in my set and we all giggled nervously as we were frog marched to Matron's office, feeling nervous and with palms sweating I entered.

A large lady wearing black with a flowing white cap sat behind her desk and peered over her glasses at us looking severe.

She told us that Nursing was a vocation and a privilege that the patient was the centre of the care and service we gave, retaining confidence and dignity in all that we did. We swore on oath to this.

I now felt like a real nurse wearing a proper uniform. The first three months would be spent at Coventry and Warwick Hospital which was residential and where I had to complete a preliminary training course. There were nurses from Nuneaton, Coventry, and Rugby who came together to do this basic training course. Needless to say we all became good pals and got up to all kinds of mischief.

SEVEN

PRELIMINARY NURSE TRAINING

PTS was quite serious, partly because of Mr Fenn the tutor, who was strict and had little sense of humour. We knew we had to knuckle down and pay attention in class but once off duty we could break free.

Lessons included practical procedures on how to give injections, bandaging, bed making, lifting and handling of patients and setting up trolleys for various treatments.

We visited the gas works and stood on top of the gas storage domes, we went to the local sewage works and drank the filtered water at the end of the filtering process to show how pure it was; I wasn't too sure after seeing the effluence arriving and going through the filter beds.

A visit to the tip showed us how rubbish arrived, was sorted and disposed of. The purpose of these visits was to highlight environmental issues and give us a better understanding of services which support health.

Other lessons included jive sessions carried out in the classroom while Mr Fenn was out. I was the teacher but unfortunately he came back early and caught us, demanding to know who the ring leaders were. Obviously no one confessed so the whole class was sent to Matron for a severe telling off.

The jive sessions continued in the common room when we got off duty until the radiogram fused, I thought I knew how to put a new fuse in, the result was that I blew all the electrics in the nurse's home.

There was always a plethora of boys hanging round the nurse's home waiting to make a catch; two of us made friends with two of the boys and went for a walk along the canal path.

I was wearing a hooped paper nylon petticoat and feeling glamorous when the hoop started to work its way out, I subtly pulled it until the whole thing came out and discretely threw it into the canal feeling embarrassed.

There was a strict door locking policy at night to make sure we were all safely in. Needless to say the curfew got broken by a few of us, not just me. We looked out for each other to ensure we didn't get caught; sometimes it meant we had to climb up the drainpipe to get back in.

The three months went quickly and it was sad saying farewell to those who weren't coming back to our hospital, but lasting friendships were made.

EIGHT

REAL NURSING BEGINS

Returning to the George Eliot Hospital meant that real nursing now began. Three months would be spent in each ward to gain experience in medicine, surgery, male and female geriatrics, paediatrics, orthopaedics, gynaecology, accident and emergency and theatres.

It was mind blowing coming to terms with how much there was to learn. I wondered if I was up to the task and felt apprehensive.

Shift patterns on days were seven thirty until four thirty, or one until ten; with just half an hour for lunch. Night shift was nine thirty until seven thirty. I thought "that is a long time to be on my feet".

The Nightingale wards held forty eight beds, in the middle of the ward were coal fires which were eventually taken out.

The days always began with ward cleaning, beds and lockers were pulled out, tea leaves which had been saved from the giant early morning tea pot were spread on the floor to settle the dust and we all swept, polished, cleaned the lockers and replaced everything. The bed wheels all had to be facing the same way. Tooth mugs were collected, occasionally with the teeth still in situ. I said to my colleagues "I thought I had come to start nursing not to be a cleaner."

My first placement was Lydgate, men's surgical. Feeling somewhat shy I was supervised shaving both faces and pubic regions often being ridiculed by the men to "mind what you do with that razor, Nurse."

Patients would be in for appendectomies, hernias, gastric ulcers, bowel blockages, cancer, kidney stones and many other conditions. Patients requiring plastic surgery were also nursed here, often after being injured following traffic or colliery accidents.

I remember a young man who severed several of his fingers after a motorbike accident. The surgeon was rebuilding part of his hand; there was a huge amount of deep bruising, so he ordered leeches to be used. I collected them from pharmacy and scooped them into test tubes. They made me squirm and I didn't want them to latch onto me. They apparently bite into the skin until attached and suck blood until they are full and then fall off, relieving the blood clot under the skin.

At the bedside David shouted, "You're not using those buggers on me I'll put up with the bruising." He took a great deal of persuading, but I got them attached and left them to have their fill, when I returned one of the "buggers" was missing much to David's and my horror. I did eventually find it among the bed sheet, much to our relief.

The theatres were quite a way from the wards so, with a porter, I escorted the patient to and from them. There were no recovery wards then as there are now and it felt quite a responsibility pushing an unconscious patient back in all sorts of weather. There was only an open sided cloister to keep the rain off and, if it was stormy, patients and nurses got wet. It was always a great relief to get safely back to the ward.

There were no such things as disposable plastic syringes, they were glass and had to be boiled in a steriliser with the reusable steel needles. After regular use, hooks developed on the needles which had to be filed down. They were stored ready for use in surgical spirit in a metal tray.

My third placement was night duty on Amos Barton men's medical ward. I was beginning to feel more confident and knowledgeable but nights messed up my social life.

Night Sister visited the wards each night to do the rounds; we were expected to know the patients diagnosis, treatments and history even if it was our first night back after time off.

One night after lights out a green cloth covered the centre light to dim it so patients could sleep and after all the jobs had been done we'd sit under this light writing reports and keeping an eye on patients.

When I looked to the top of the ward I noticed a red glow keep appearing then fading. It was creepy; nurses had mentioned a ghost being seen on this ward so I felt nervous but went to investigate. As I got closer I smelt smoke then saw a patient with an oxygen mask on attached to a large free-standing oxygen cylinder happily puffing away on a cigarette.

"What on earth do you think you are doing?' I roared, "You could have blown yourself and the ward up." He was none too happy when I confiscated his fags.

I was planning to go dancing with friends on my next night off so thought I would wash my hair while on duty, we didn't have hot running water at home so it would be quicker and easier and I could go straight to bed in the morning.

Night Sister usually came around the same time so did it in my break, a colleague keeping watch suddenly knocked on the bathroom door "Perry she's on her way I can hear her coming," she whispered. Night Sister had come early.

"If she asks where I am, tell her I wasn't well. Give me time to rub my hair dry I'll be out as soon as I can." Panicking, I furiously rubbed my hair with the towel and put my cap back on.

Thankfully she had begun the round which gave me a few minutes then I began to feel water trickling down my neck and my cap feeling limp.

Then she came to me "What's the matter with you Nurse Perry you're looking rather flushed."

"I wasn't feeling too well, Sister, it's that time of the month." I lied," I'm just going to take something for it."

"Well, you'd better, Nurse, you still have work to do. And do something about your cap it's a disgrace."

Then she trotted off to the next ward. I'd had a lucky escape

I was a rather clumsy nurse; the shoes I wore were heavy leather black lace ups. To make them last longer I had steel toe and heel studs put on them which made them noisy and slippery.

While rushing into the ward kitchen I slipped and crashed into a fire extinguisher, setting it off. Foam sprayed everywhere. Fortunately it was a warm summer's day and the window was open so, hoisting the extinguisher shoulder high, I aimed the jet of foam through. It reached the ward next door and sprayed through their window too, needless to say I became the laughing stock of the hospital.

I was severely reprimanded by the ward sister "Nurse Perry you must really try to be more in control. You cause havoc around this place breaking things and dropping things. And get some shoes which make less noise, you're a disgrace."

I don't know how she thought I could afford new shoes, I was only earning fifteen shillings a week and most of it went on board, bus fares and stockings and most of those had laddered and been sewn up so much that they looked as if they had tram lines up them.

Strict discipline was the order of the day especially in regards to punctuality. I depended on buses to get to and from work and they were few and far between with none running on Sundays.

One thick freezing foggy Sunday I could easily have rung in sick but decided I daren't. Unable to see far in front of me I proceeded to cycle the eight miles to work, hitting the kerb a few times, eyebrows and nostrils freezing up and eyes streaming.

I arrived at the hospital just as the fog was lifting, approximately ten minutes late, I had to ride across the courtyard in front of Home Sister's office.

Before I'd reached the ward she had summoned me to tick me off. Without taking my coat off and ice clinging to my eyebrows and the hairs up my nose, jaw and lips feeling fused, I tremulously made my way to her office.

"Nurse Perry, what is the meaning of you coming to work late, didn't you think you would be seen arriving through the fog? What if all the nurses decided to come late, night staff unable to go home and there would be no one to nurse the patients. I shall report you to Matron."

I could have easily retaliated but bit my tongue, humbly trying to apologise. I wished I'd stayed at home like many other nurses did.

It was still foggy when time came to go home.

Mum was waiting up, worried about me on the bike, I relayed what had happened. "I'm going to give it all up if that's how they treat you, I could have been killed for all she cared. I wouldn't mind but I did make an effort to go and that's all the thanks you get."

Mum made me a welcome hot cocoa and said, "Look, you needn't pay me board for a few weeks, go to the motorbike shop in Nuneaton and see if you can get a second-hand scooter."

The next time I went I called at the shop to check the prices. They were between fifteen and thirty pounds so, after chatting to the owner telling him that I was going to get one soon I went home excitedly to tell Mum.

It was quite a while before I'd saved enough to purchase the

Lambretta I had set my heart on, so continued meanwhile to travel by bus and to cycle on Sundays.

One Valentine's Day I received a card. I had no idea who this person was – I was flattered and excited to get it and was itching to know who he was. All it said was "from Jim, an admirer."

Everywhere I went; on buses, to dances, to village activities, to the pictures in the next village, I wondered if anyone was looking at me just in case 'Jim' would make himself known to me.

One Saturday morning while waiting at the bus stop, an old van pulled up and a good-looking young man stopped. "Can I offer you a lift to work? I'm going past the hospital." His face was familiar; he had thick black wavy hair. Grateful, as the bus was late, I accepted.

"I'm sorry I've only got an old van, but it gets me to work and back."

He seemed quite shy, but told me he was a carpenter and joiner and he worked at the Jaguar car factory in Coventry. He knew my name and said he had seen me on the buses coming home from work.

"How do you know my name and what's your name?"

"It's Jim and I've admired you for a long time, but didn't dare pluck up courage to speak to you."

I was beginning to get goose bumps. I asked him," Did you send me a Valentine's card? It was from a Jim and I don't know any other."

"Yes, I did. I hope you don't think I'm silly," he said.

"Yes, I was very pleased to get it as I've never had one before," We reached the Hospital; I thanked him and got out.

"Perhaps we'll see each other around sometime," said Jim as he drove off.

Some time elapsed before I saw him again. I threw myself into studying, then one day I saw him at the village garage, filling his new car up with petrol. He and the car looked very smart. Very dishy.

Jim came across the road to talk to me. "Would you like to go out for a drink or to the pictures or perhaps choose something else if you like?"

I thought I'd finished with boys, but Jim had been on my mind since our last meeting. He was shy and quietly spoken but was a gentleman, so I agreed to meet him.

We went to the pictures and then to a café. We chatted for ages getting to know more about each other. Jim had four sisters and two brothers. I was one of six children, so we had a lot in common. This felt like the start of something good and the beginning of a lasting relationship.

Training was progressing well, although stressful and hard work, especially all the exams which, thankfully, I passed first time.

Accident and emergency was intense; casualties arriving from colliery incidents and explosions. The men were often traumatised and had severe injuries as well as smoke inhalation.

Frequent motorbike casualties arrived, some looked as mangled as their bikes must have done, often with deep lacerations and fractured femurs which required pin and plating and a long hospital stay.

Regularly on a Sunday night an elderly lady who fainted in church was brought in. To examine her, with great resistance, many layers of clothes had to be removed; vests, liberty bodices, corsets, bras, and more bodices. In between all of these layers was all her wealth, notes galore.

This money had to be counted by two people and secured in the hospital safe.

It was no wonder she fainted, I don't think her lungs could expand.

Friday and Saturday nights heralded the arrival of the drunks. If they were unconscious they were admitted to the orthopaedic ward, where the resident patients were none too sympathetic. They thought it was disgusting that nurses had to look after them.

Often there were stabbings, even one of our own nurses was stabbed as she was coming to work, and her lung had collapsed.

She had a police guard outside her ward, thankfully she made a good recovery.

At Christmas there was a tramp who repeatedly tried to feign illness to get into hospital for his Christmas dinner. We called him Bill Sykes.

My last placement was the operating theatre. I was now twenty years and six months old with six months left of my training.

I wasn't too sure whether I would enjoy this or not but I absolutely loved it, a great deal to learn, the names of all the instruments to start with.

Pam Gupwell a staff nurse was my mentor and we clicked immediately. She had a wicked sense of humour; she took me through the instrument cupboard teaching all the names prior to Sister Carter testing me. "Ok Nurse Perry, let's see what you've learned."

I began, "Spencer Wells, Vulsellum, speculum, artery forceps, abdominal retractor and whoopee clip."

"I beg your pardon, Nurse, what did you say?"

I repeated, "A whoopee clip, Sister."

"It's a penis clamp, Nurse, now let's proceed."

Guppy, laughing, thought it was hysterical.

The operations we did were hernias, appendectomies, caesarean sections, kidney stones, nephrectomies, amputations, gynae ops, abortions and plastic surgery.

Sometimes, if patients bled, the surgeon would call for a bowl of ice cubes to be brought in; a large swab was soaked in the ice-cold water and placed on the area to stem the bleeding.

I was the nurse fetching the equipment one day. Rushing back with the ice cubes I skidded and dropped the lot, cubes and steel bowl bouncing and clattering on the concrete floor, me sitting in a puddle of ice cold water with a very red face and Mr Dencer, the plastic surgeon, glaring over his glasses at me.

I did live it down eventually.

After a full day two of us would sleep in at the hospital to be on call for any night emergencies. Often there would be two or three cases.

In theatre we had to do all our own sterilising, scrubbing and boiling instruments, laying trollies with all the right instruments, scalpels and sutures, washing and powdering gloves, filling the drums with gowns and towels and ensuring they were sterilised and ready the operating lists.

If there was spare time we rolled cotton wool balls and made gauze squares from a giant roll of gauze and then sew twelve squares together ready for the ops.

Like the instruments, any multiples which were used were in sets of twelve. They were counted before and during the op; as they were discarded they were hung on a rack and counted again prior to the surgeon closing the abdomen to make sure all were accounted for.

One evening, after all our jobs had been done, Minnie Chin, a Chinese student nurse who was full of fun, and I decided to pierce my ears. We had talked about it and she had a spare pair of sleepers which she loaned me.

"Okay, Perry, let's get started." She'd set a trolley up as if she was going to perform major surgery.

I lay on the theatre table and she sprayed local anaesthetic on my ears but it ran inside and froze my ear drums. "Oh, Minnie, what have you done?" I screamed in pain. It scared me, I thought I'd gone deaf and jumped off the table.

The effect wore off quickly so, after stuffing cotton wool inside my ears, we had a second attempt and were successful. I felt chuffed to bits as all my friends had had theirs done and I was the last.

My relationship with Jim was flourishing and going from strength to strength. He insisted on coming to fetch me from work when I was on the late shift, which was lovely and meant I got to see him more often.

I was really falling in love.

NINE

HITCH HIKING

My sister, Pearl, was headstrong, creative and artistic. She had an American boyfriend, a soldier who was stationed in Germany. Desperate to find him she arranged with her friend Cynthia to go hitch hiking through France, Belgium and Germany where she could finally get her hands on him.

She had registered with the Youth Hostel association and had received maps and details of where the hostels were situated. This was the cheapest way of travelling as neither of them had much money.

Pearl announced to Mum what they were planning. She was worried and shocked at the idea of two vulnerable girls travelling abroad to foreign parts with little money, no knowledge of the language or culture; she thought it was a dangerous idea.

In spite of Mum's protestations, Pearl was determined to go – but Cynthia changed her mind and backed out. Being stubborn and ignoring Mum's pleas, she said she would go on her own.

Mum, feeling desperate, appealed to me, "Christine, you'll

have to go with her or she'll go on her own." This was the last thing on my mind.

"I'm not going, I'm not cut out to go hiking all over the world, besides I want to stay here with Jim."

I was in love and didn't relish a walking holiday with my stroppy sister. I wasn't built for hiking and couldn't bear the thought of leaving Jim behind for ten days.

My conscience got the better of me when I saw how troubled Mum looked so agreed.

The day arrived for us to leave, laden down with rucksacks and a camera borrowed from Sonia, my younger sister, and we set off. Neither of us had a proper pair of walking shoes.

Jim drove us to Watford Gap services on the M1, where I said a tearful farewell to him. We caught the train to London and then on to Dover. We hadn't even walked very far before I had blisters.

At Dover, we used the ladies room then walked towards the ferry when I noticed Pearl hadn't got the camera or jumper. "Where is the camera and Sonia's jumper?" I shouted.

Rushing back to the toilets she discovered they had been stolen.

I couldn't get excited about this holiday and felt thoroughly miserable whereas Pearl was ecstatic about going to see Norman.

Thankfully the ferry crossing was smooth and we landed on French soil at Calais. This was my first trip abroad so I thought I might as well try and make the most of it, I just wished I could be as enthusiastic as Pearl.

Armed with a map and phrase book we began trekking through golden cornfields. It was late summer, and the ears of corn were ripe ready to pop. Thankfully there was a welcome gentle breeze.

We reached a dusty cart track which made it difficult to walk, grit getting into our shoes cutting our feet and making them even more sore.

We meandered through open meadows, sprinkled with an

abundance of wild flowers pink clover, blue corn flower, and deep reds of poppies.

At the corner of some of the fields was a small canopied shrine containing statues of the Virgin Mary and Baby Jesus.

I wasn't a Catholic, but it was comforting, being miles from home, hungry, tired and not knowing where we were or where we would sleep. I did say a little prayer or two for our safety and that the walking would get easier.

We called at farmsteads along the way and in a dismal attempt to speak their language using our phrase book we asked for water to fill our water bottles.

People were very obliging, not only giving us water but food, drinks and fruit and inviting us in to rest. They were interested to learn about us too.

It was getting toward evening when we reached the main road and managed to flag down a car which took us to the nearest youth hostel.

This was nothing more than a small rather dilapidated sports pavilion, inside was sparse with rickety, damp, dirty bunk beds with sagging mattresses.

We were greeted by two Dutch girls who had arrived earlier they spoke good English which to me was a joy to hear. "Welcome my friends, this isn't the best of places, don't let it put you off. There are some beautiful hostels; we'll tell you where to go." They were well equipped and obviously had hiked before, they loaned us their flea powder to put on ourselves and the beds.

"I can't thank you enough, the thought of sharing a bed with fleas makes my skin crawl" I said grimacing, to which they just laughed.

Feeling exhausted, I would have gladly slept anywhere, and thankfully we had our own sleeping bags so felt a little bit more cosy and protected.

I awoke to the smell of bacon cooking, by now I was starving and knew all Pearl and I had got for breakfast was bread and cheese, but our Dutch friends generously gave us a bacon roll each. We were very grateful, I savoured every mouthful.

Setting off early we were back at the main road and soon got a lift in a lorry, there was room in the cab, so we climbed aboard. I always let Pearl get in first and sit next to the driver; she was braver than me.

After driving quite a distance he stopped in the middle of a motorway to let us out, not too sure where we were we carried on walking when we suddenly heard sirens.

A police car pulled up and made us get inside, they gave us a good telling off "Do you know you are breaking the law, walking isn't permitted on the AutoRoute, you could be killed." They took us to their station, I was convinced we'd be jailed and was terrified, Pearl was more confident.

After checking our passports, reprimanding us some more they gave us a welcome cup of tea and pointed us in the direction of the railway station.

The next youth hostel was near the station on the French border. It was an improvement on the sports pavilion, even though dormitories and showers were communal; there was at least hot water.

Meals were provided which usually consisted of hard rolls with jam and cheese and strong sludgy coffee. At least it was better than nothing. I was grateful for anything.

We decided that as soon as it was morning we would take the train and cross the border into Belgium. All Pearl could think about was getting to Germany, and Norman, as quickly as possible.

All I could think of was how homesick I was and how much I was missing Jim. I couldn't wait to get home.

Brussels was beautiful; wonderful architecture, especially the fountain with the small boy peeing. I brought a postcard of this to send to Jim and decided I would write letters to him regularly.

A pleasant man with a posh car stopped to talk to us, "Where are you heading girls, I can see your travelling light, can I give you a lift?"

Pearl, taking charge and showing him the map, said, "This is the youth hostel we are trying to get to, just over the border in Germany. We'd be grateful for a ride if you're going that way"

"I will be going in that direction later; I have business to attend to first. Go and get something to eat and I'll meet you back here at the car in two hours." He gave us some money and the keys to his car. I was amazed at how trusting he was, usually I felt suspicious of everyone and this was the reason I preferred to sit in the back of vehicles and allow Pearl to take charge and sit in the front.

Finding a market selling vegetables, Pearl tried to communicate with the seller. She asked for two tomatoes and put two fingers up to demonstrate. He issued us with two kilos, not wanting to seem rude we took them.

Bread rolls and tomatoes tasted real good.

True to his word, the business man returned, and our journey continued. We headed for the border where he dropped us off. Hailing another lift, we managed to reach Cologne.

The youth hostel here was at the back of a library, the facilities were quite a better standard although there were still bunk beds and coffee was still strong. People of various nationalities stayed here.

Itching to get to Nuremberg where Norman would meet us, we tramped hard through medieval towns of Rothenberg, Frankfurt and Wiesbaden to reach our destination which was right at the top of a hill overlooking a cemetery.

A castle with a moat around loomed in front of us. The warden looked like the Hunchback of Notre Dame; he carried the biggest bunch of keys on his belt. "Give me your cards, you must sign in," he bellowed while looking meanly at us. This place, we learned, had belonged to the Hitler Youth Movement. When we tried to find our cards we discovered that we had left them behind at the last hostel, I began to feel threatened by his attitude and wondered if he had been in the Gestapo. "No cards, you can't stay," growled the warden. He was refusing to let us in until another nicer younger deputy intervened. "We can ring the last hostel to check their details, we can let them in". Reluctantly he allowed us in.

I was relieved as I was fed up, tired, hungry and my feet were throbbing and blistered. I couldn't wait to kick my shoes off and soak my feet.

The showers were inviting and quite an experience. They were enclosed in glass in a big circle in the centre of the room with fountains of water spraying out. Uninhibited other girls stood naked in front of them washing.

No way was Pearl, and certainly myself going to expose ourselves in this way. We retained our dignity by showering in our bras and pants.

There was a pay phone in the hostel, Pearl wasted no time in contacting Norman to say we had arrived, he would be coming the next day. She was ecstatic and wouldn't shut up about him.

I was thoroughly miserable and felt lost and lonely. I did a lot of crying, Pearl constantly reminded me. I took comfort in writing another love letter to Jim, I hoped he hadn't lost interest in me in my absence.

Pearl was in her element now; she would be seeing Norman. She had been getting on my nerves constantly talking about him; she kept telling me off for mentioning Jim and how I was missing him.

The next day, Norman arrived to be met by Pearl fluttering her eyelashes looking coy and trying to be sexy. They did a disappearing act to find somewhere isolated where I imagined they would waste no time getting passionate.

I went off for a walk around the castle to take in the view, there was a bench where I sat looking over the cemetery feeling sorry for myself fed up and desperate. Thinking about the corpses buried there.

Eventually Pearl and Norman reappeared looking hot and bothered, Norman was going to take us for a meal which was a bonus although I felt like a gooseberry.

We went to a fish restaurant where all kinds of fish were swimming in a large tank. We had to choose which we wanted, and they were killed and freshly cooked.

While I didn't like the idea of murder, I was too hungry to object so thanked the fish silently and ate heartily. It made a real change from the meagre monotonous meals we had been having.

Norman took us out for the next couple of days and one evening, dancing at a night club, I had to admit he was a gentleman, considerate and a good looker.

I tried to make myself as scarce as possible to give them time together before we had to make tracks on our homeward journey.

It was now Pearl's turn to feel miserable and unhappy.

Norman gave us a ride as far as he could then it was thumbing lifts again and getting as quickly as we could back to Calais and the ferry.

We made friends with a pleasant young Indian boy on the Ferry who spoke good English. "Where have you been and where are you going?" he asked eager to learn.

Pearl told him in detail and I chipped in when I could find a gap, although she didn't stop to draw breath very often.

He brought us cups of coffee and a bun each and told us, "I am going to Birmingham to visit my uncle and cousins; it has been a long time since I saw them. I might be coming to live with them."

We arrived in Dover exhausted and slept on the pebbly beach for a couple of hours, counting our money we had only eight pence left.

Heading for the main road, the young Indian man stayed with

us. He spoke to a bus driver, checked where he was going and if he would give us a lift. He himself was going to the railway station.

The bus was empty "Choose which seat you want girls there are plenty to pick from," he said cheerfully and off we went.

After some distance, he pulled into the services to get a bite to eat. "Come on then girls let's take a break, we'll be here for a while and then I'll take you further."

Knowing that we only had eight pence, Pearl said "It's alright thank you, we'll stay here until you're ready."

"You've not got any money, have you? Come on I'll get you something."

We didn't need to be told twice as we didn't know when we would next eat or when we'd get home.

He drove us as far as the nearest underground train link and bought us a ticket each to get to Watford Gap where our journey had begun. I know I felt a great sense of relief.

After Watford we managed to get a lift with a man in his car. It seemed everything was going fine until it broke down and he had to call the AA.

I could see them in conversation, pointing to us and laughing. When the car was repaired the driver went on his way, the AA man said "Jump in I'm taking you home." He took us all the way to our door.

I was so happy to be home at last I dumped my rucksack, kissed Mum on the cheek and said, "I'll sort my things out when I get back I want to go and see Jim, be back later."

During the two whole weeks away from home I had thought a few times of Mum's safety and if my siblings were alright but being so far away meant there was little I could have done. Now, back here at home, the anxiety returned.

Mum said she had been fine; seldom did she say anything else, she was always stoical trying to protect us, but the tension in the atmosphere said differently.

The anticipation of the weekends; Dads trips to the pub, returning drunk and the resulting violence reared its ugly head once again.

The third step of the stairs became a familiar zone to sit and wait for the fights to start, they nearly always did.

TEN

MARRIAGE

Sonia, my younger sister, now had a regular boyfriend Fred Beaufoy. He was a biker and their relationship was serious, she was planning to get married and was only seventeen.

Pearl threw herself into another relationship, I think she realised Norman was too far away to develop anything that could last. This boy was a twin called Duncan Woolerton.

Jim and I were getting closer, although he was quite shy, it was a while before he kissed me until one night, saying goodnight in the entry at the back of the house, we were just holding hands I said "It's alright if you want to kiss me, I won't bite".

I didn't have to say it twice, from then on he didn't need my permission, but he was always a gentleman.

My brother, Duncan, was also getting serious with his girlfriend, Pat. I think we were all looking for opportunities to get married to escape our situation and I worried that everyone would have tied the knot before me.

Back at the hospital my training continued. I was managing

to pass all the exams which I had to study hard for but was still surprised to have passed first time.

I received an invitation to attend a prize giving. I thought it was just to be in the audience. I was told I had to go in uniform, imagine my surprise when I heard "Sister Tutors prize for practical nursing is awarded to Christine Perry" I don't know how I managed to stand let alone walk up to collect it. I had never been awarded anything in my life before and was ecstatic. The prize was a text book Tooheys' Medicine for Nurses.

It was while working in the operating theatre I took my final exams. I had spent six months there and, after qualifying, was offered a post which I accepted eventually spending two and a half years there.

During this time Pearl and Sonia had married. I said to Jim "Isn't it time we started thinking about marriage?" He had never suggested that we got engaged; I couldn't wear rings at work so wasn't too bothered but was eager to marry.

"We'll see what we can afford next March and think about it." This was twelve months away so, with a relish I chose the bridesmaids, booked the chapel, chose my dress.

Together we sorted the invitations out and I notified the Registrar which I had to pay seven and six for. I always told Jim "I think I was good value for money even though I'd paid it myself".

The reception was to be held at the village social club which was run by my dad's sister, Auntie Ethel. The local ladies who mum was in the Civil Defence with offered to cater and wait on us. We chose ham salad and tinned fruit and cream, the cake was made by my friend Connie Summers from the Young Farmers group I went to.

While I had thrown myself into the planning I had real misgivings about Dad giving me away. He had paid nothing towards it and I didn't relish walking down the aisle on his arm or even being sociable with him, but knew I had to make the best of the situation and grit my teeth.

The day arrived sunny, the wedding planned for twelve noon, everything appeared to be going to plan. My brother-in-law, Arthur, was driving guests to Chapel in his Riley car. He came for the bridesmaid in good time, then there was a delay.

Twelve fifteen, Arthur pulled up, "What's the problem?" I shouted through the front door, neighbours were queueing up in the street to watch me leave.

"The Registrar hasn't arrived; it seems he's forgotten. The Vicar has contacted him, he's got another wedding at two o'clock and he'd not put yours in his diary. I'll pop back and see what they've suggested."

I couldn't believe it after all our planning. Dad, trying to be cheerful, said "Never mind, who's this Elizabeth Taylor they all talk about?" I suppose it was his attempt to say something complementary.

Arthur reappeared, "The Registrar said we are to go ahead with the service, he's on his way and you can repeat the vows when he arrives." It was now twelve forty.

I rushed out to cheers from the neighbours, who had been bending their ears to find out what was going on, and got to Chapel.

Dad immediately trod on my veil and tore it, frantic guests who had poured outside rushed back inside. I grabbed Dads arm and flew up the aisle to stand beside Jim, who was looking a bit strained.

I was thinking about the food at the reception of dried up ham, curled up bread and lettuce caused by the delay, then Jim squeezed my arm and I re– focused.

Reverend Churchward explained about the vows, and the service commenced we went outside took a few photographs, confetti and rice was thrown, we were getting into the car to go to the reception when a tap came on my shoulder.

"Can you come back inside the Church, I need you to come

and repeat your vows." It was the Registrar who looked as if he had just got out of bed wearing a crumpled suit and shirt.

The remainder of the wedding went well; we visited Grandma Price who had dementia and was in a long stay hospital to give her my bouquet and then set off on honeymoon to Newquay in Cornwall, staying the first night at The Kings Head in Cirencester where we had the Bridal Suite.

The bed was a huge four poster, I had to almost do a running jump to leap onto it, it was so big. I won't tell you what happens next you can use your imagination.

The wedding had taken a big chunk of our savings, affording a house or even rent was difficult, so for a few months we stayed at Jim's home, paying a small amount for board and saving hard for a deposit for a house.

Through a workmate of Jim's at the Jaguar car factory in Coventry, we learned about the new houses being built in Cosby and that their prices were much more reasonable than at Coventry.

We went to visit the site and look at plans. As there were only a few left we decided that enough was saved for a deposit. There were only a few left, so we picked a house; number 11 Hill View Drive.

This felt very grand and exciting, but I had some reservations, I said to Jim, "It seems a lot of money we have to save, are you sure we can afford it."

The house would cost three thousand five hundred pounds, and would take a year to build. Jim said, "It's ok, we've been agreed a mortgage, we're both working it will be fine."

Slightly reassured, we went home to share the news. Shortly after, I discovered I was pregnant. I worried about money, the cramped conditions at Jim's house as we only had a small bedroom and the length of time to wait for our own house to be finished.

We moved back to my house where there was a larger front room which we turned into a bedsit. It also meant that I could keep an eye on my mum and younger sisters as things hadn't improved. My brother, too, during this time got married and moved out.

I continued to work although shifts were tiring; I had acquired the scooter, a Lambretta, while living at Jim's to help make travelling easier. It cost fifteen pounds and we saved on the cost of bus fares. I picked it up at the shop, had one lesson in the street and was off. It felt exhilarating.

Being second hand it was a bit battered, scratched and temperamental but it got me to work and back and allowed me some spare time that I wouldn't have had waiting around for buses.

Saturday, June thirteenth at twelve ten pm, after forty-eight hours in labour my first baby girl was born at the George Eliot hospital Nuneaton, in the middle of an horrific thunder storm.

I thought she was never going to come but she arrived safely although she had a squashed nose as she was facing the wrong way.

It was strict visiting on the ward, husbands only and half an hour allowed in the afternoon and evening. Jim couldn't get in the day as he was working extra time to save for the house and he was late coming on that Saturday evening.

I was getting angry feeling sorry for myself and highly emotional; when he came into the ward I shouted "where have you been I've been waiting all afternoon to show you your daughter and you're late".

He looked sheepish and pulled a bunch of five red roses from behind his back "I've been to get these for you they cost one and five each and I only had enough for five,"

After a good cry I told him I was grateful and sorry to have been annoyed and gave him Louise to hold, it was a name we had both agreed on.

I returned home to Mum's house with mixed feelings; excitement with Louise, raised emotions, getting into a routine, breast feeding but also worry about the ongoing situation between

Mum and Dad, it hadn't improved even though Jim was present, especially weekends when Dad came home drunk.

I couldn't wait for our house to be completed, the builders were dragging their feet as we weren't able to get over to visit and push them along more quickly. Half of me wanted to escape, the other to stay and be the protector.

I kept busy making curtains for the lounge, bathroom and nursery. Mum had taught me how to use her treadle sewing machine and I had made baby night gowns too.

I took Louise for long walks in the white silver cross pram. It was a high pram, well sprung; I had brought most of the baby equipment second hand from a workmate of Jims.

One day I pushed her to the shops and parked her outside, did my shopping and walked home, forgetting her until a neighbour stopped me and said, "Haven't you had that baby yet you must be well overdue." I was wearing a baggy coat that I'd worn throughout my pregnancy and obviously still looked pregnant.

I didn't stop to answer and rushed back at top speed feeling very guilty.

October 1964 the house was ready. We had been buying some second-hand furniture, an Ercol dining table and chairs had been stored at my sister's house, a large double bed and wardrobe we'd brought from a family in the village where I used to baby sit. And we had saved to buy a new Ercol settee.

I said "Jim, are we going to hire a removal van to transport everything, so we can do it all in one go?"

"No, I've already arranged with Vick, my brother in law. He's lending us his van, we can make several journeys and it will save money."

I had passed my driving test when I was four months pregnant. It had been a struggle to get behind the steering wheel even then, I had come off night duty, straight into a lesson and then into the test so was feeling tired.

I think the examiner took pity on me as I was still in uniform. During the three point turn I hit the kerb twice, when asked to turn left I turned right, at the end he said "We have time to spare; perhaps you would like to try another three point turn and do it properly this time".

I couldn't believe it when he handed me a certificate to say I'd passed.

So, when we moved into our house I was able to carry a lot of things as well, not forgetting Louise.

Jim made three trips in the van with the help of Vick. It was on the final lap that the suspension began to make strange noises; probably it was a good thing that everything had been transported before it gave up altogether.

It felt bitter sweet being further away, leaving Mum, Rosemary and Wendy behind and yet still feeling euphoric about our home.

It was magical hanging curtains, making up beds, installing everything in its rightful place, having a proper bathroom with cold and hot running water and not having to ladle it from a copper, putting clothes in drawers and wardrobes.

It was brilliant cooking a meal just for ourselves and using our own crockery and cutlery, and sitting at the table which took pride of place in the dining room.

I hadn't got round to finishing the curtains for our bedroom, so on the first night we tacked a large sheet up to the window, Jim had had his bath and was snuggled up in bed.

I had my bath and ran into the bedroom naked, as I'd left my nightdress in there, when suddenly the sheet fell down exposing me to the street. I turned the light off quickly only to be illuminated by the street lamp straight opposite the house. I think the neighbours saw more than they had bargained for.

It was so lovely having all the space and being able to please ourselves after being cooped up in the front room at home.

Louise had her own nursery and settled in very well. A contented baby with blonde, almost white, wavy hair, we established a routine quickly. Bathed her, fed her, and put her into a nightgown ready for Daddy to come from work, play for a while and then settle before we had our evening meal which was timed to perfection.

The table was set, meal cooked ready to serve. I tried all sorts of recipes; now that I could branch out and be adventurous in my own kitchen I was in heaven.

We used Terry nappies for Louise. I would be up early to see Jim off to work at the Jaguar car factory in Coventry and then I'd get the washing done.

The washing machine was a twin tub Rolls Royce which we had bought by paying in instalments. We agreed that we would only buy one essential item at a time, pay it off as quickly as we could, and not get into debt.

The nappies were boiled until pure white, spun, rinsed and spun dry again. My greatest pleasure was being the first in our row of houses to peg them on the line and see if mine where the whitest. Most of the neighbours had children of similar age so it almost became a competition.

The first Christmas in our home came. I was almost delirious thinking about how I would decorate the house, what we would have to eat, what should we buy Louise and each other.

I had made Christmas cakes and puddings, pickled onions, pickled cabbage, mince pies and shortbread; even Irish cream containing whisky. The smell of pickles penetrated the house and lasted for days, but it was such a feeling of satisfaction to have made them all.

Louse was now six months old getting very knowing. Christmas Eve, having got her settled in bed, she was fast asleep when I heard carol singing and bells ringing, I called downstairs, "Jim have you got the radio on? I can hear carols."

"No, I haven't, I think it's coming from outside. I'll go and look."

He went outside and came running back in excitedly, "Quick, look through the window, Santa's outside on his sleigh."

I ran and looked out, sure enough there he was. I dashed into Louise's room picked her up and, trying to wake her, dashed to the window hoping she would see it and enjoy the spectacle, although she did seem rather bemused.

It was such a glorious, happy feeling which made me feel warm inside. After settling her down again I went downstairs to Jim and reflected on how lucky we were.

Christmas day tea time and we were going to visit Jims' family. It was a long-standing tradition that the family all got together on this day. Jim was one of seven children, three of his older sisters who all had children would be there and his two younger brothers.

His father was a miner and they lived in a colliery house which overlooked the pit and the pit bank. They loved celebrating Christmas and you could hardly see a space on their ceiling which wasn't covered in decorations.

His dad always shopped on Christmas Eve and brought a large jar of sweets each just for the ladies of the family. I felt very privileged to be given one.

I looked at how different the relationship was between Jim's mum and dad; loving affectionate and joyful. It filled me with sadness to reflect on how things were between my own parents. I couldn't help wondering what their Christmas was like, although we were going to visit them before we went back to our own home.

I felt pretty torn; not wanting to leave this happy celebration to go to Mum's, not knowing what might be happening. It felt like a constant cloud hanging over me and a feeling of dread at the back of my mind.

At least I could hopefully cheer them up when we got there to give them all the presents I had made and brought.

My eldest sister's family lived in a flat in the stable block at Caldecote Hall, a mansion house at Nuneaton. She had two children. She had heard that a small flat was available to rent.

The situation between Mum and Dad was escalating and having an effect on my two younger sisters. So, a decision was made for Mum to apply and, if successful, as a family we could move them into the flat.

Thankfully she got it and, while Dad was at work, we all rallied together, grabbed what we could filling old cases, a tea chest and making sure we took her sewing machine we made a quick escape.

It felt terrifying and exciting at the same time trying to avoid gawping neighbours, worrying that Dad would come home early and catch us doing the deed and getting everything into the car.

There was some hilarity too, although I think it was nervous giggling, but the thought of removing them to a safer place spurred us on.

Mum had stayed at Caldecote to look after the children while we transported her belongings, unpacked and arranged them in her own little flat.

It was fun and hard work carrying everything in having to climb four huge steps and open massive doors while lifting boxes. Duncan shouted, "Come on our Christine, we can lift this chest we've got plenty of muscle between us."

We hoisted it out of the car boot. I walked in reverse, climbed the steps but there was no one to open the doors. I said, "Hang on to it a minute Dunc, I'll just open the door, it won't take a second," and I left him hanging on, taking all the weight and going red in the face. "Who the bloody hell do you think I am, Tarzan?" he called as he dropped the whole thing spilling the contents down the steps. We burst into fits of laughter, thankfully it wasn't raining.

The flat was small with windows in the flat roof, one bedroom, a kitchenette, a bathroom and lounge where Mum's bed had to go.

We tried to make it look cosy and pretty with a few ornaments and a bunch of flowers.

We couldn't wait to see their reaction. When they walked in it felt quite emotional, even though Mum seemed wary. It was a massive thing for her and all of us, not knowing what repercussions there might be.

The girls, however, were happy but somewhat bewildered to move into a new home, they had visited Pearl here on many occasions and loved the space, the grounds, and the woods where they could play and have freedom.

Mum loved Caldecote. It had its own tiny church which held some services and she planned to join the local parish church at Weddington too.

Rosemary, who was fourteen, continued to attend Arley Herbert Fowler School although it meant she would have to travel on two buses to and from school.

Wendy, who was nearly five, had to be registered at the local Weddington School.

They all settled in very well, and everything appeared to be going smoothly, when Mum became ill. She began having psychotic episodes which frightened the girls, she was imagining there were men on the roof with guns. They fetched Pearl and called the doctor and Mum was sectioned and admitted to Lichfield Psychiatric Hospital.

She was an inpatient for many weeks and had to undergo electro convulsive therapy (ECT) to help to stabilise her as she continued to hallucinate.

I suppose the trauma of her life of abuse had taken its toll.

It was a very worrying time for us all. Pearl took Rosemary and Wendy under her wing and cared for them in her flat. I visited and did what I could trying to share some of the responsibility.

I visited Mum every Wednesday at the hospital taking Louise with me. I was six weeks pregnant with our second child, during this period it felt stressful as this was the day Mum had her ECT.

It was traumatic and sickening watching how the treatment affected her. She sat rocking backwards and forwards, her face flushed with a glazed expression. She didn't respond to my conversation, it was an awful time, but we had to accept it was necessary for her to get better. Eventually she did come home but wasn't in any fit state to care for herself or the girls. Pearl continued to do all she could. I took them to my house during holidays as much as I could, and Sonia and Duncan did their share too.

It took a lot of persuading and cajoling to get her to the point where she could take responsibility again and they moved back into their flat, only for her to relapse again and be readmitted. This time she was allowed to come home but had to attend once a week as an outpatient to have more ECT.

Mum objected to being collected by ambulance for these appointments so I travelled over to pick her up and take her to the ambulance station and she would then go and I collected her on her return.

They stayed at Pearls for some time and, thankfully, Mum gradually recovered.

Mr Coburn, the owner of Caldecote Hall, was looking to appoint a housekeeper for his own apartment. A flat was offered with the job, Mum was interested and applied, was successful and so we all became removal men again.

Thankfully, Mum's stability continued for quite a length of time, although Rosemary felt lonely as she was missing her friends from Ansley Village. Wendy was fine as she played with Pearls children who were similar ages.

Our relief was tangible, while everything seemed to be going smoothly again, we all hoped and prayed it would stay that way.

Life moved on more smoothly, pregnancy developed without any hitches and Beth arrived in the early hours of Thursday morning on the sixteenth of February 1966, weighing seven pounds, a good home delivery.

It was a textbook birth, hardly any pain, no effort required to push, and she just slithered out. I even said to the midwife, "Shall I try to push her out."

Nurse Worsley said, "I don't think you need to, she is already here." I couldn't believe how easy it had been.

Louise and Jim brought me coffee and toast in bed. She was fascinated with Beth's tiny fingers and toes; it was a delight to watch her reaction.

Not long after this, Jim learned that he was being made redundant from Jaguar. They were making lots of cuts and sadly he was one of them. I thought things were too good to be true. It was a real shock.

He didn't waste much time finding another and secured a job with Rentokil, treating wood worm, dry rot and dealing with pest control. He had to travel over quite a big area for this business and often came home late.

We continued to enjoy the family, the house, developing the garden and inviting friends and family for meals.

Birthday, Christmas and New Year Eve parties were a success, relatives came from Nuneaton, Ibstock and Bedford, we played daft team games, dancing and had lots of fun and laughter. There was always plenty of food too.

On New Year's Eve we did the conga up the street where occasionally neighbours joined in, it usually ended with me being lifted up and dumped in the conifer bush in the front garden.

Our son, Andrew, was born on March twenty eighth 1968, weighing in at nine pounds. It was not quite as easy as delivering Beth as the cord was round his neck. Nurse Worsley was brilliant; she should have been off duty but was still with me until five to twelve when he arrived.

I said that Andrew looked like the image of my dad.

During this confinement I had thought more about my father and the relationship that there should be between children and their grandparents. I vowed that I would try to rebuild my relationship with my dad although I couldn't forgive him for what he had done to Mum.

The next day my brother called to congratulate us on Andrew's birth but also to let me know that my dad had died. He had cancer of the oesophagus and had been in Hospital for some time.

Jim was over the moon at having a boy, he himself was the first son after four daughters in his family so was eagerly awaited as was Andrew.

I decided that now our family was complete.

ELEVEN

JIM'S HEALTH

I knew when I had met Jim that he had health problems. A heart condition caused by rheumatic fever when he was eighteen had triggered weak heart valves and a degree of heart failure, but he had recently been discharged from hospital to the care of the GP, saying that he was ok.

It came as a shock when Andrew was just six months old that Jim's condition deteriorated and he was admitted to Leicester General Hospital suffering from Endocarditis a severe bacterial infection of the lining of the heart.

It was extremely worrying as he didn't respond to treatment immediately, when I visited the hospital the doctor called me into the office to warn me that if he didn't respond to treatment that night he could die.

As a last resort they were going to inject antibiotics directly into his heart. I could only try to be brave, not let Jim see how upset and concerned I was and wait and pray.

All I could think of was our three young children being left without their father, I don't know how I drove home that night.

Our very good neighbours had heard of our plight and between them they had organised a rota to sit with the children which allowed me to visit Jim. I will always be grateful to them.

Then the good news came via a telephone call to say that Jim had turned a corner and was responding to the treatment. The relief was immense. He spent a further six weeks in hospital then came home on bed rest but wasn't allowed back to work for a year.

As he hadn't been with Rentokil long they only paid him for a few weeks, money was becoming short. There had been little time to put any savings away so, with some reservations, we applied for benefits, only to be refused initially.

While Jim was convalescing, the GP suggested he might try some light work to see how he coped. I sanded down the ground floor window sills and Jim began painting them when an official from Social Services arrived with his big folder under his arm.

He introduced himself loudly and then said, "My good man if you can paint windows you can go to work and shouldn't be asking for benefits."

I thought Jim would have a heart attack, after all he had been through this was the last thing he needed. It had taken all his pride in the first place to ask for help and he told the official this in no uncertain terms.

He did eventually back down and complete the forms and we were given a little help.

Christmas was here again, this time we had to be very sparing. I made glove puppets, dresses, sweets and cakes. I was feeling subdued and thinking that I should get a job to help to pay the mortgage as we had only been paying off the interest due to Jim's health and we weren't too sure when he would be fit for work.

On Christmas Eve a knock came at the door. Opening it there stood a lady, a neighbour who was an ambulance driver; she was holding a big box of goodies, "Here you are Christine, we've been delivering Christmas parcels to patients and just have this one to spare, Merry Christmas." With that she turned and left.

I was dumbfounded. It was full of treats, chocolates, tinned fruits, biscuits, meat, cream and all sorts, I felt very humbled.

Then there came another knock at the door. It was Pam, a neighbour; she brought a little wooden rocking horse for Andrew, a dolls crib for Beth and a small house tent for Louise. "They are second hand but have been restored and painted and new covers made for the crib, we just wanted you to know we are thinking about you and hope they cheer you up." I burst into tears at such kindness and couldn't thank her enough, it was truly an uplifting humbling feeling I couldn't describe. The children loved their presents and I was so touched and grateful for such kindness shown to us during a very tough time.

TWELVE

COSBY LIFE

Life moved on. Jim was off work for a year; although he was frustrated he made good progress and found things to do. He enjoyed attempting cooking, helped around the house vacuuming and dusting and playing with the children.

Throwing myself into village life, I began helping at the play school, making cakes to sell for their funds. I joined the young wives and got involved with taking some sessions.

A speaker had cancelled at short notice, I was contacted to see if I could fill in and demonstrate to the group; the theme was crafts for Christmas. I was the least crafty person you could imagine but agreed to have a go.

Jim had some books on crafts so searched them for ideas. Out of a cocoa tin I made a dispenser to hold scissors, string and pens. A large cardboard box I turned into a clown with an open mouth into which you threw balls of screwed up paper. Other items were made from cardboard.

Feeling nervous, knowing full well there would be people there far more creative and qualified than me to demonstrate, I set off. While loading things into the car there was a sudden downpour of heavy rain. My treasures, which had taken three whole days to make, were now wilting.

Arriving at the hall I gingerly carried them in, destroying them even more, and put them on the table in front of everyone.

With a dry mouth and feeling just a little bit sick I began by describing exactly what these items were. "These crafts I so lovingly made require just a little bit of imagination, I will circulate pictures so that you may see what their function really is."

There was some laughter from around the room, but I wasn't going to wilt like the creations. "I apologise for the state they are in, it's not due to my handiwork but the weather. I invite anyone with any other ideas to come forward and save my bacon." I was feeling very embarrassed at this point. But nearly everyone joined in sympathising and sharing ideas. At least the cakes I had brought didn't end up a soggy mess and were enjoyed by all.

I joined the Cosby Amateur Dramatic Group who put plays and shows on at the Bunning Hall, they also wrote scripts and music for their own pantomimes. I made all the costumes for Aladdin and played the part of Nefertiti. The sewing machine was in our bedroom which didn't please Jim too much, but he tolerated it for a few months. After visiting a few material factories in Leicester to see if I could beg some of their waste, Leicester Pleating gave me samples of beautiful fabric still on rolls. There was enough on one to make stage curtains and the pleated nylon was perfect for costumes.

The local dancing school including our girls took part; they all looked cute in the thirty green elf costumes which I'd made.

I had begun to think about getting myself a job, Jim had returned to work but came home exhausted and his health was a worry and unpredictable.

Nurse Worsley, the midwife who had delivered Beth and Andrew, had become our friend. On one of her visits she said, "There is a part time District Nurse post going to be advertised at the Northfield Doctors surgery, it was for three hours a day from Monday to Friday. I just happen to have an application form if you're interested." She knew I would be as we had chatted about it, it was a gift.

I sent the form off to County Hall and was called for interview. I had given a lot of thought to child care, my next-door neighbour who ran the village play school said, "I can take Andrew to play school with me three mornings a week if you are successful."

Another friend, who was a child minder, said, "I have spaces if you want me to have him for the other two days."

I could hardly believe how everything was falling into place; it was too good to be true. Louise and Beth were both at school so they would be fine and should I get the job I would be home in time to meet them out. I was feeling very blessed.

Miss Wright, the Director of Community Nursing, conducted the interview. She was a jolly chubby lady; a midwife. Her main concern was our arrangements for the children which I explained. There were two of us to be interviewed, I was first and was asked to wait outside until the second was done.

After what seemed like forever the other interviewee came out and left, I was summoned back into the office and told, "You interviewed very well, and I'd like to offer you the job. The contract initially will be for three months, come with me to another room I'll get your uniforms."

In this room she climbed a ladder laughing and chattering and kept throwing uniforms down from the top of a cupboard, "Here you are, try these on. See if any fit you." Trying to be discreet I tried them on. Then, pulling her skirt up, she said, "I wear these they are so comfortable," as she stretched the leg of her Playtex panty girdle. "They are supposed to make you lose weight although it hasn't worked very well for me yet."

What a revelation! I hadn't expected that but went home full of excitement to break the news to Jim that I was starting work.

I hoped it would all work out well and that Jim would feel less pressured.

THIRTEEN

DISTRICT NURSING

I met with all the members of the practice, who were very welcoming, and began my induction into district nursing with Nurse Worsley, who was a combined Midwife and District Nurse.

The villages we covered were Blaby, Cosby, Narborough and Broughton Astley. I ran a morning surgery and then did community visits which included some residential homes.

Treating patients in their own homes was very different to hospital care. You were dealing with the whole family, had to be adaptable, and remember that you were a visitor.

I felt nervous and excited at the same time, Nurse Worsley spent a month with me and then I was on my own.

There were many conditions to deal with, stroke patients, patients with Alzheimer's, cancer, shingles, multiple sclerosis, amputations, post– operative patients, and children who had appendicectomy or circumcisions, just to mention a few.

The mornings passed quickly, and it wasn't long before I felt accepted. Nurse Worsley had been attending many of these patients for a long time and was a hard act to follow, popular and highly respected, so I was unsure how I would be received.

I was asked if I would consider doing my District Nurse training and think about increasing my hours, but I didn't feel the time was quite right although arrangements at home had worked well and the children hadn't appeared to have suffered in any way.

Jim was seen regularly at Groby Road Hospital and, following one of his cardiac catheter tests, his aorta was found to be leaking and becoming incompetent. He was only thirty one and this operation wasn't done at Groby on young people so he had to go to London to the National Heart Hospital. The thought of this was terrifying to me, Jim was anxious but seemed to accept it. A pre-op trip to London for another cardiac catheter showed that the aortic valve needed to be replaced. The date was set and we came home to make plans. I felt completely torn; do I stay here with the children or go to London to be at Jim's side? Who could I get to care for the children if I did? I couldn't bear the thought of Jim going through it on his own. I was given three weeks compassionate leave so if things could be arranged it would be possible to go with him.

Pearl, my sister, said, "We'll take the children, we have the room and we can arrange for them to attend the school that ours go to." Feeling highly emotional I hugged her and shed a few tears, I was so grateful. I explained to the children, "Daddy has to go to London to have an operation on his heart and Aunty Pearl has said you can stay with them at their home in Ibstock, "how do you feel about that if I go with Daddy?" They shrieked with joy. "Yes, please, will it be like going on holiday? Will Uncle Duncan tell us ghost stories in the cellar and will we be able to play in the attic?" They loved going there and had spent lots of time with their cousins, it was decided that they would stay there for the three weeks; my prayer had been answered.

The children excitedly settled in at Pearl's the day prior to us leaving for London. I hoped they would be ok, I knew they would be happy there but still had nagging thoughts.

The dreaded day dawned, and we caught the train. All sorts of thoughts were running through my mind but I tried hard to make light of the situation to keep Jim's spirit up.

FOURTEEN

LONDON

London seemed vast, noisy and busy as we made our way to the hospital. It did nothing to distract from the sick feeling I felt; inside my stomach tied in knots.

We were escorted to the ward where Jim was made comfortable and I arranged his belongings in his locker; a photograph of the children I placed on the top.

The formalities of form filling, explanation of the operation, what to expect and the signing of the consent for surgery was carried out, this made it all seem final and frightening.

The operation to replace the aorta valve using the pulmonary valve and replacing that with a pig's valve was quite a new technique designed and developed by a consultant Donald Ross, hence it was called the Ross procedure. It was also called the Homograft.

We were told that Mr Ross himself would be performing the op and felt privileged and fortunate. Jim would also be put on a by-pass machine, where he would be put on ice to keep his body temperature low.

I asked Jim, "How do you feel about all that's going to happen, is there anything you want to say or ask?"

"No, not really, I just want to get it over with and get back home. How long do you think I'll be in?"

Jim was always a man of few words, where I was desperate to ask lots of things but didn't want to cause him to feel any more anxious so kept quiet. I suppose the nurse in me needed to know all the technical details.

I was given a room to stay in the hospital for four nights free of charge and it was reassuring to be close by. The hospital had an arrangement with a Church Army hostel on Marylebone Road where I could stay afterwards. This was run by nuns. The charge was quite low which I was thankful for as money was still quite tight.

The morning of the op dawned. I hadn't slept much, I don't know about Jim.

I was allowed to see him briefly prior to being taken to theatre. He was a bit drowsy having had his pre-med, I just wanted him to know how much I loved him and I wouldn't be far away.

I had been asked to stay close to the hospital just in case I was needed so sat for a while in the reception which looked out onto the street. After about an hour a large black saloon pulled up and I watched a small man emerge, "Good morning, Mr Ross," the receptionist said.

"Good morning," he replied.

After he had gone I asked, "Is that the Donald Ross the Cardiologist?"

"It sure is, and he's a real gentleman and a clever doctor, but he has to stand on a box to operate as he is so small"

I learned that he allows the teams of surgeons and doctors to get the patients prepared and on by-pass and then he arrives to do the actual repair. I also learned that sixteen units of blood were required.

Thankfully I wasn't summoned during the op, which took about five hours so, to me, that meant it had gone to plan. He was sent to recovery on a ventilator for four days.

I was reassured that it had gone well and I could pop in briefly later in the evening to see him. I couldn't wait to see for myself that he was ok, even though I knew he would be on a life support machine.

He looked very pale with a long incision down the centre of his chest and two electrodes sticking out each side of his wound. These would be used to give an electric shock should his heart stop beating, which was somewhat worrying.

I squeezed his hand and kissed his forehead and went to my room, relieved that he had come through but knowing there was a long way still to go. I fell on the bed feeling weak and trembly and the tears came.

I was feeling sorry for myself, missing the children, worried about Jim and finding London the loneliest place to be; no familiar faces and no phone at hand to contact anyone and hear a comforting voice. I hoped the night would go quickly so that I could visit him again.

Feeling desperate, I fell to my knees and prayed as I'd never prayed before. I heard a voice say to me, "No news is good news, get into bed and go to sleep." It was such a comfort, so I did as I was told.

The days seemed long and lonely. I was missing the children and needed to find something to fill my days and occupy my mind. I thought that my training must stand for something.

I spoke to Matron, "Is there anything I could do or anywhere I could help in the wards or the hospital to pass the time away?"

She replied, "You could be useful helping on the children's ward, reading to them and playing with the children recovering. There are often jobs like hand washing more delicate clothes that aren't sent to the laundry, I'm sure there are things Sister can find for you to do."

I wouldn't be allowed to do any nursing and nor would I want to, anything to fill the time in between visiting Jim would be a relief, although she said it wouldn't be wise to be there every day.

Matron took me to the ward, these poor sick little mites either waiting for or recovering from heart surgery. It didn't seem possible that they could survive yet survive they did. I was amazed at their resilience, their fight and determination, and how quickly many of them bounced back.

If these little ones could make it then I was more hopeful that Jim would too.

Jim made slow and steady progress, I couldn't wait for him to be taken off the ventilator and be able to hear him speak again, the four days he was on it seemed like forever. The first thing he said after coming off was, "Hello love are the kids alright?" It was great to hear; they were and always had been his first priority.

He was feeling groggy for some time, then began to fight back. He was allowed to sit out but hated having physio where they pounded his chest and made him cough to clear it.

I did feel I could begin to relax a bit and decided I needed at times to escape the hospital environment, so wandered around the local streets. I managed to afford to pop in a nearby café and felt civilised again but knew I wouldn't be able to afford it too often. I tried a Rum Baba cake for the first time; it was literally soaked in rum and was a luxurious treat.

I could have visited museums and art galleries, which would have filled some time, but it hadn't occurred to me that they were free, so stuck to wandering the streets; sitting on park benches with tramps and alcoholics and generally take in my surroundings.

People watching became a fascination, conversations with tramps were enlightening and revealing. One gentleman with a straggly beard and hair, surrounded by his worldly goods in plastic bags, asked me as I was sitting silently beside him, "Are you alright my dear you look lost and pre-occupied."

I was stricken with how well he spoke and replied, "I'm fine, thank you, just a bit forlorn and lonely," I proceeded to tell him why.

He told me, "I've been living rough for many years but had to escape from the rat-race. I had a good education, job and home life but felt trapped and couldn't cope with the pressures so left it all behind."

I wondered what the lives of all the other rough sleepers I saw might have been like; it certainly gave me something to think about.

I was thinking about the children and how I would like to take a little gift home to let them know I had been thinking about them. There were many small shops selling London memorabilia; magazines, papers, cigarettes and unusual items.

Spending time in one, I was looking for the cheapest items. I picked a giant pencil with a union jack rubber on the end for Andrew.

I spotted small boxes containing a figure of the Madonna. Feeling sentimental and emotional I thought these would be just right for Louise and Beth to stand beside their beds. Taking one out to examine in more detail, I fondly handled it when I noticed some men in the shop laughing at me. I looked more closely at the figures and saw the words "The answer to a maidens prayer" written on it. Turning it over in my hand I discovered that it was shaped like a penis.

Needless to say I did a quick disappearing act.

After four days I moved to the Church Army hostel on Marylebone Road next to Madame Tussauds.

This place was clean but sparse. The rooms contained a bed, chair, table and sink, the bed linen sparkling white and starched stiff. At least it was somewhere to rest my head.

The nuns were quite strict; breakfast at seven am, rooms evacuated at nine thirty and not allowed to return until after six pm. This didn't bother me too much as I would be visiting Jim.

After two weeks, Jim was moved to convalesce at a Little French Hospital on Shaftsbury Avenue – it was much further to walk. As I was having to budget carefully, I walked everywhere in the day then caught a bus back to the hospital in the evening. This felt safer too as I felt quite vulnerable.

One early morning as I walked through an underpass following what I imagined was a gentleman – bowler hatted, smart black suit, briefcase and umbrella– he suddenly stopped in front of me undid his fly and peed up the wall. I couldn't believe what I had just witnessed.

Another day as I sauntered along I was conscious of a man following me. Every time I stopped or popped into a shop he stopped and was there when I came out. This went on for some time and made me feel scared and that I must be cautious.

I had heard about all the theatres in the West End and, on one Saturday afternoon as I slowly meandered along Shaftsbury Avenue taking in the sights, I found myself looking at the theatres thinking how splendid they looked and how great it would have been under different circumstances to be here and see a show.

I was working my way towards the Hospital as it was near visiting time when I felt someone grab my arm and continued to walk along with me, he was a small but smartly dressed man who spoke with an accent and said, "You German? You have somewhere to stay?" I wasn't sure how to react but replied, "No, I am English and I have somewhere to stay on Marylebone road." "I can offer you a room if you need one, here is my card and number," he continued to grip my arm. "Where are you from and why are you visiting the Capital?"

"I'm from Leicestershire and my husband is here in Hospital." I was feeling sick and afraid and pulled his hand away and managed to break from him.

Fortunately, I was at the hospital entrance so dashed in and ran upstairs to get away. I realised he must have been a pimp and I could have been one of his victims. I must have appeared a good catch in my summer clothes, white shoes and matching shoulder bag.

I sat in the waiting room trembling and trying to compose myself before going in to see Jim. I felt I'd had a lucky escape; I was desperate to share this dreadful experience with someone but knew I couldn't tell Jim even though I was longing to be comforted.

I realised I was going to have to be more vigilant and aware of everything around me and not let my guard down for a minute.

Jim was making good progress and had made friends with several other patients especially one young man from Derby. They got on really well, but sadly he relapsed and passed away. Jim was grief stricken and became low for a while. The good news was that if he continued to do well he would be allowed out for a day, so if I could manage to get the children up to London to see him I would.

My three weeks in London had come to an end. While I was desperate to get the children home, I was torn knowing that Jim would still be stuck in hospital. But there was no choice.

We said our tearful goodbyes and I left him to go and catch the train, assuring him that I would be bringing the children the next Saturday and I would ring the ward as often as I could.

The children were excited to see me, although Louise was tearful, she had developed a painful abscess on her back. She had fretted – being the eldest she felt responsible for Beth and Andrew. I suppose it had taken its toll. The hugs they gave me were wonderful.

Thanking Pearl and Duncan I said, "I will be eternally grateful to you for helping us out I don't know how to thank you." Pearl hugged me saying, "Thanks aren't necessary, they have been good and had lots of fun, we're just happy that Jim is recovering."

It felt strange arriving home for all of us but it didn't take long for them to settle in and race to get their own familiar toys and games out. They couldn't wait to see their friends.

At bedtime and after their baths while sitting on their beds I spent time talking to them, "How are you all feeling and are you glad to be home?" I asked.

Beth said, "Is Daddy going to die, will his heart break?"

Louise replied, "No, of course he's not. they're making him better in hospital."

Andrew was too young and pre-occupied with his toys to even enter the discussion until I said, "On Saturday we are going to go on a train ride to visit Daddy at the hospital and you can see for yourselves that he is getting better."

"A real train ride, all the way to London! How many sleeps 'til then?"

"First you have to go back to your own school, you can tell them all about your adventures at Aunty Pearl's and Saturday will come very quickly. Now it's time for sleep."

It was wonderful having them back, although I couldn't stop feeling anxious about Jim all on his own miles away.

Saturday came; the children woke early falling over themselves with excitement, "What are we going to do when we get there?"

"What is it like on a train?"

"How long will it be before we see Daddy"?

They nervously got on the train and we were off. I was tense, making sure that I didn't lose any of them, especially when going on the underground.

Fortunately, the station wasn't far from the hospital, and we went to the ward. There were lots of tears from all of us as they hugged Jim.

Beth couldn't stop staring at the long scar down his chest. "Why has Daddy got a ladder up his chest," she asked. The pacing wires had been removed, thankfully they hadn't been required, and I would have worried about Andrew giving them a tug had they still been in place.

The nurse said, "Ok, Jim, you can go out for the day but must be back by five o'clock where would you like to go? We'll order a taxi but be careful and don't over exert yourself."

I suggested the zoo at Regent Park. It wasn't too far away as I had walked there on one of my previous walks.

The weather was good so off we went. It felt strange being given freedom – even though it was only for a short while I couldn't help feeling anxious and responsible for Jim's well-being and was amazed at how well he coped having been cooped up for such a time.

It was a treat to see the children happy and it reassured them that Dad was going to be alright, the zoo was a real success. I had taken a picnic to save money but bought drinks and ice cream.

All too soon time was drawing to a close. We hailed a taxi and got back just in time.

Back at the ward the nurses greeted him like a friend we said our goodbyes again and took a taxi to St Pancras for the journey home. It wasn't long before they were rocked to sleep by the motion of the train and I could peacefully reflect on what a day we had just shared.

We repeated this trip once more before Jim was finally allowed home. I wanted him home but after having such a major operation I was concerned as to how frail he might be during his convalescence.

I needn't have worried as he was stoical, determined, never complained and took it all in his stride which was a relief to know that he would be alright while I was at work.

Back home we slipped into daily routines. I took the children to school and together we would walk to pick them up and take them to the park. Jim passed time reading, resting, experimenting more with the cooking. The dinners he made were delicious, he cooked meat and sausages mashed and roast potatoes, numerous veg and extravagantly made sauces adding cream if it was available.

At least we were all eating well. I think he used every pot, pan and utensil in the kitchen which I then had to wash up.

I didn't mind, it was just so good to have him back and see him getting better.

Rentokil were keeping his job open, which was a relief, although he wouldn't be returning for some time.

I now had to agree to do my District Nurse course, which meant I would be full time. Thankfully, all the children were at school, so it made it possible, while Jim was convalescing he could meet them out of school. Friends had offered once he went back to work, plans were always having to be made.

The course was held at Charles Freer College in Leicester, a beautiful house bequeathed to be used for nurse training. We attended some sessions at Scraptoft campus.

The downside was that it meant I had to move areas and leave the Northfield practice. I was sad to leave them as they had been so supportive but there was no choice as my post had been filled.

I would now be working at Narborough Health Centre for Dr Orton, Swallow and Millac. I needn't have worried as they were very welcoming and friendly.

I was given a caseload and was mentored by another nurse/midwife Margaret Lang, who showed me the area and introduced me to the patients. She did visits with me on a regular basis to supervise and observe and write reports which were then submitted to Miss Smith, my tutor at college.

They were a good friendly bunch of nurses from all over Leicestershire. One of them, a real animal lover, arrived one day with a small box. Every two hours she opened it and fed milk from a doll's bottle to a baby shrew which her dog had unearthed. Sadly, her efforts were in vain as it didn't last long, I was pleased she didn't attempt the kiss of life.

I passed my course and was raring to go. I learned that I would be staying with Doctor Orton's practice which was a relief as it was nearer to my home and meant I could manage to get home in my lunch break if only briefly to check on Jim.

The patients were lovely and pleased to learn I would be staying. My area covered Blaby, Cosby, Narborough, Broughton Astley, Dunton Basset, Croft and Potters Marston; beautiful villages to drive through.

District Nursing was a privilege – to be welcomed into people's homes was special and were some of the happiest moments of my career. It wasn't always without difficulties or problems.

Accessing patients' houses in the 1960s– it felt a safer time, so keys were hung on string through letter boxes. It didn't always work, as confused patients would cut them off. Some refused to answer their doors; one elderly lady who refused so we had to call the police to help. It was a wet day, in front of the house under her windows were waste bins, a young policeman climbed up to open a window wider to reach inside and suddenly the lid gave way and he was up to his waist in water. The lady then decided to open the door.

Another time I called and let myself in with the key on a string. There was no sign of her and we'd had no instruction from family that they were taking her out. I searched the whole house went through the kitchen, out into the back garden. As I came back in the pantry door flung open and there she was, naked. "Boo! I could hear you looking for me," she chuckled and trotted off. Needless to say I responded "You silly little woman you could have been lying injured or dead somewhere, don't ever do that again."

Another time I had to reach over a gate to unlock it and run for the back door to unlock it to avoid the geese who charged at my legs.

I was bitten by dogs on several occasions; an off licence I called at the door was ajar and as I put my arm through a huge Alsation wrapped his jaw round my arm. Fortunately I had my thick winter coat on, so he did little damage.

Health and safety wasn't as strict then as it is now; hoists were just beginning to be introduced into the community.

The kind of conditions and treatments we gave were varied and many, patients with cancer, severe shingles, strokes, blood disorders, amputations, caesarean sections, post-operative conditions, diabetics, leg ulcers, eye drops and injections, enemas and many others.

There was no division between nursing and social care in the sixties and seventies, so a day could include getting coal in, making fires, boiling water, preparing food and drinks, emptying commodes and making beds.

Home helps were provided by social services, we also could obtain medical aids like wheelchairs, beds, commodes, air mattresses and urinals from the Red Cross – these helped to make our work a bit easier.

There were always plenty of leg ulcers, sometimes they would heal and then break down again. There was one lady who had an ulcer, when we unwrapped the bandage there were maggots inside. It wasn't too pleasant but surprisingly the wound was quite clean.

One of my favourite challenges was being asked by the Hospital A and E department to assess for care an elderly blind and deaf lady who had fractured her arm and was badly bruised.

I called at the house; the neighbour had the key and went in. She was sitting in her armchair, it was obvious she had been neglecting herself, was rather dirty, coal slack everywhere, a woolly hat on that was matted to her hair and was in a lot of discomfort.

Having to shout to introduce myself as her hearing aid wasn't working properly; I told her who I was.

The neighbour said, "I try to help and bring her meals but she's very independent and won't let me get help or do anymore for her. I'm at the end of my tether at what to do."

Gladys started crying, "Don't send me away, you won't send me away will you Nurse?"

I said, "Look, Gladys, if you accept our help we can come in to visit you, get you a home help and you can stay here. We'll need to order you a bed and do something to make it safer. I'll start by giving you a strip wash and check you over will that be alright?"

"Yes, please, as long as you don't send me away."

I boiled some saucepans of water, checked in her cupboards and drawers for clean clothes. When I saw mouse droppings among them, I found some flannels and soap and began. "Do you mind if I remove your hat and cut your hair?" I asked.

"No, do whatever you have to do but please don't put me away."

I had to trim her hair which was attached to the hat and tried to make it look as neat as possible. I then washed it and towel rubbed it dry.

After undressing her I could see how bruised she was and proceeded to give her a good strip wash, cutting her finger nails which were long and grubby.

The last thing after putting her clothes on was to wash her legs and soak her feet. The nails were so long they curled round and dug in, part of my equipment included special clippers for nails.

I knelt down to cut her nails when I spotted movement across the room and saw a big rat followed by smaller ones walking towards where her pantry was.

I gritted my teeth and carried on keeping my eyes peeled and managed to cut them they were so hard they shot across the room.

She looked lovely when I'd finished, she cried and said, "I feel beautiful, Nurse, thank you, thank you."

I felt a real sense of achievement and very humbled too, but I had to tell her about the rats and mice. I said, "I'll contact environmental health who will come in and get rid of them and social services will send a home help to help you clean and shop and we'll order meals on wheels, and nurses will come to help you each day, how does that sound, Gladys?"

There was no objection and she accepted that she needed help.

She is one of the patients I remember fondly.

Another was Harry, who we used to wash and help dress. He was a belt and braces man and wore long johns. One day I attended to him, the next day he said "What was wrong with you yesterday, Sister?" I asked, "Why what was the matter?"

He said, "I've been going round in circles for the last twenty-four hours trying to find my willy you put my long johns on back to front."

At Christmas I would prepare dinner early at home, put the turkey in at five am and Jim would put the potatoes, stuffing and vegetables on to cook at the right time while I was at work .

When I came home I plated up three dinners to take to patients before we had ours. The children insisted on coming with me and they had wrapped a little present for them and took a cracker, one was for Mrs B who was blind and lived alone, she was sitting at her table with her knife and fork ready, and was excited to open her present and pull the cracker but was eager to tuck into her dinner.

The others were for an elderly married couple who struggled to get about. The children had to sing a carol to these and they were eager to eat their dinner too, they were delighted we'd taken apple sauce.

The children often still talk about it.

One day while driving home I passed a house and saw a man lying face down by his gate in his driveway. He appeared to be rolling and twitching so I stopped the car and dashed over, with a pull I got him onto his back, in his hand was a hand trowel. "What the bloody hell?" he yelled.

"Oh dear, I thought you were having a fit." I replied.

"I'm not having a fit I'm digging a hole for a bloody gatepost."

With that he got on with his digging leaving me feeling stupid and embarrassed. Especially as I had waved Nurse Worsley down, who was just passing, to give me a hand?

The funniest thing I discovered was what patients use their incontinent bed pads for 1, to keep car engines warm in winter.

2, to put around the skirting boards when decorating. 3, to absorb condensation around window sills. 4, to line the bird cage.

These are just some of the joys and delights of being a District Nurse.

FIFTEEN

CONTINENCE ADVISER POST

I was developing signs and symptoms of osteoarthritis, my hands were painful and X-rays showed that the middle joints had crumbled. Surgery was necessary to fuse the joints to reduce movement and relieve pain.

It came as quite a shock but I had been finding some nursing procedures difficult, it made me wonder if my nursing days were over.

I went in for surgery to have the ligaments lengthened and steel pins put in until the joints had fused into a functional position. I was off work for five weeks. The right hand was done first, the left hand done straight after.

I pondered all this time what my future held as it wasn't going to be easy going back to district nursing.

While convalescing, still with pins and stiches in, I was suddenly summoned by the Director of Nursing for the community to discuss my future. I really thought it was to be sacked when she said, "Well, Sister Hall, I have a proposition to put to you. You won't be able to go back to practical community nursing, your hands won't allow it."

I was stuck for words wondering what she was going to suggest, "What do you have in mind Mrs Grove?" I spluttered. I really was happy being a District Nurse, loved the patients and the area I covered and didn't really want to leave it behind.

"You're not on the scrap heap yet, I want you to train to become a Continence Adviser. Go and do some courses, work alongside the Continence Adviser and the clinic at the Leicester General hospital and learn from Professor Castleden, the Geriatrician who has a special interest in the subject.

"You will be the first Continence Adviser in the community, how do you feel about that,"

I felt out of my depth, not happy about change, but could see that she had given it a great deal of thought and I had been given a life line.

"Do I have to decide today, or can I think about it?" I nervously replied.

"Let me know by next week, you have a free hand to design a service, we'll support you all the way, come and talk it through and we'll get you on a course. There's a conference in London you are already booked on"

A week later I stood in front of her and accepted.

After the pins and stitches had been removed and some physiotherapy my hands adjusted to their new position, with some fear and trepidation I tried to focus on the challenge ahead.

I entrenched myself in studying, reading, developing ideas attending clinics learning how to perform Cystometry, collecting samples of continence products, liaising with company reps and continence advisers from other areas. I attended a six-week course at Selly Oak hospital in Birmingham; it was a massive learning curve. So much to take in.

I came up with ideas of how to move the service forward and how to utilise the resources we had. The community was huge so knew I had to disseminate information to, and use, other nurses in developing a service.

Mrs Grove was true to her word, I saw her every month to share ideas, plans and feel supported. I had been based at the General Hospital for three months attending a weekly clinic and eventually running one of my own, taking patients from the community. But there was resistance from the existing staff there that there wasn't enough room for me, so I couldn't stay there.

It was decided I would be peripatetic; stay in one health centre for three months, train nurses in that centre and establish a continence clinic. I identified individual nurses who had shown a real interest to run these clinics with my support and gave them a title of Link Nurse.

Eventually clinics were established in most health centres in the City and County.

In conjunction with Mrs Grove and Professor Castleden, I wrote an article called 'Fifty Six Continence Advisors One Peripatetic Teacher.' This was published in The British Medical Journal, The Nursing Times and The Nursing Mirror. We had enquiries from New Zealand, Australia and other places expressing interest in how the services were developed.

While developing clinics for adults it was evident that there was little available for children with problems like bed wetting or faecal soiling, so I began working with school nurses and the Paediatric Medical Officers and Judith North the team leader for school nurses, to establish these clinics too.

This change of direction from District Nursing was challenging but very rewarding. Getting nurses to be committed to promoting continence and not just providing pads was sometimes tough but the support and belief of Link Nurses and the relief felt by patients made it all worthwhile. Even though every time I appeared I was called the incontinent lady.

SIXTEEN

SHANDY BLUE

Christmas was here again; the children had been pressuring us to have a dog, so we agreed on an Old English Sheep dog. The day arrived when we were going to choose him.

The children didn't need to be told twice to get washed and dressed, they gobbled their breakfasts and we were off.

We had read books about the breed, learned they would grow big, need lots of grooming and exercise and would have a large appetite. Of course the children were all for it Andrew said, "I'll take him walks every day."

Beth and Louise said, "It's alright Mum, we'll brush him and feed him, you and Dad won't have to do anything."

We arrived at the house, they could hardly contain their excitement, the door opened slowly and out ran these little black and white bundles of fluff, nine in all, I had never seen anything so cute.

The children were on their hands and knees laughing and screaming as the pups gambolled around, falling over each other, nipping their ankles and fingers, and chewing their shoes. It was such a lovely sight, seeing them so happy.

Eventually we were all on the floor while the pups clamoured all over us biting ears and noses and making little puddles.

It took a long time to decide which to have, but at last we agreed it was the one with the big round head and large eyes who fell asleep on Andrew's knee.

We paid the lady, thanked her and set off for home. Back home the kids couldn't wait to show Shandy Blue his treats and surprises, a new bed, feeding bowls, teddy bear, squeaky toy and a blanket.

They mixed some baby cereal with milk and watched him eat it. He really enjoyed chasing his bowl round the kitchen floor until every last bit was eaten – much of it was stuck to his whiskers.

Half of the water from his drinking bowl was tipped on the floor and paddled everywhere.

At bedtime, the kids tucked him up in his blanket and gave him his teddy then tried to creep away to go to bed. They hadn't reached the first step before Shandy was out like a shot chasing after them, dragging his blanket and teddy behind, just wanting to play.

They thought it was hilarious so I had to shut him in another room so they could go to bed.

We had survived the first day. I could begin to see what was in store but he was beautiful and cuddly and I knew we would have a lot of fun even if he was full of mischief.

Shandy proved to be a handful, so strong he pulled the children to school on their sledge when we had snow, their friends were envious, and all wanted to have a go.

On the beach on holiday we sat on blankets, people in front of us were sitting around in deck chairs with their backs to us, Shandy proceeded to dig the sand from around their chairs causing them to collapse, creating mayhem but, thankfully, they saw the funny side of things.

He went running and bounding along the beach unaware of the rock pools where he suddenly did a nose dive and belly flopped into the water. It took him by surprise and he quickly retreated shaking the water onto anyone nearby.

One evening we went to buy fish and chips so left him in the rear of the car which was separated from the front by a grill, on our return the people who were parked next to us were having a good laugh. "You have a very clever dog there, as soon as you had gone he pushed the grill open with his nose and sat in the front seat, as soon as he saw you coming back he jumped into the back again, he's been very entertaining".

We had a neighbour who was small in stature whenever she called round Shandy would crawl through her legs lifting her up in the air, needless to say, she didn't call too often.

He had so much energy we decided to try to curb it a little and enrolled him into training classes; I went with one of the children to a church hall in Wigston.

On arrival the other dogs were lined up in the down position by their owner's feet, being well behaved. I managed to get Shandy to lie down but he preferred to lie on his back with his legs in the air and straining to be let free. I dreaded what might happen if I did let him go.

Next exercise was to walk in a circle, dogs at heel with the lead on, then try to get them to stop and sit. It proved quite difficult as all Shandy wanted to do was sniff the bottom of the dog in front, which the other dog objected to.

The trainer's dog was well behaved and sat on the stage behind a curtain. This changed during the exercise we then did to trust our dogs off the lead. It began with them lying in the down position while we all stood in two rows opposite each other; I could see the mischief in Shandy's eyes and knew it meant trouble.

No sooner had I taken his lead off he was like a rocket firing, chasing the other dogs and charging at the stage to get at the trainer's dog who leapt up and tore the stage curtains. I felt utterly embarrassed and ashamed and felt the scorn of the other owners.

I kept his lead on for the rest of the session not wanting to disrupt things further and making a bigger fool of myself, the trainer had quite a few words to say at the end.

"This breed, Red Setters and Afghans are the most difficult to train and the most scatty you won't do much with him until he's about eighteen months old, you can try again and bring some treats like cheese or biscuits to give as rewards."

The next week we were going to do some retrieving work and dumbbells were required so thought I would try again.

I told Jim how we had got on he saw the funny side of things, and being a carpenter, he said, "I'll make him his dumbbell it won't be difficult." And off to the garage he went.

The next session I went armed with a pocket full of cubes of cheese and biscuits and his dumbbell which I thought did feel heavy but took it anyway.

I felt a bit more optimistic and seemed to be making a little progress, although the cheese and biscuits were disappearing quickly and Shandy's nose was almost permanently stuck by my trouser pocket.

It was now time to throw the dumbbell. Other dogs did brilliantly and fetched theirs on one command. Their equipment wasn't heavy, made of light plastic which didn't make much noise.

I got Shandy to stand at heel and threw his dumbbell which clattered and rolled until it hit the stage with a loud thud; it was twice the size of the other dumbbells. "Fetch." I shouted, he looked at me confused, "Fetch." I tried again, no response.

I began to run and shouted "Fetch Shandy, good dog." he ran beside me. "Bring, give." I appealed and moved his dumbbell which he tried hard to pick up and eventually succeeded it was so heavy he trotted off with his head hanging to one side swinging it in his mouth and slobbering.

I decided dog training was too much like hard work we persevered for several weeks and gave it up, vowing to work hard when we took him for walks ourselves.

It was spring, and we decided to lay a lawn thinking it would be easier to keep tidy, somewhere for the children and the dog to play, we spent time preparing the ground making it level in readiness for ordering the turf.

With interruptions from the children and help with digging from Shandy it took us a whole day to do plus another day cleaning the mud from the kitchen floor where they had paddled. I prayed it wouldn't rain before the turf arrived.

With the grass piled neatly we began, Shandy keeping a beady eye on the proceedings. It all went down and looked beautiful, it seemed a shame to even walk on it, the garden was transformed.

Going indoors for a well– earned cuppa and a rest it seemed rather too quiet. Shandy had stayed outside. "He can't come to any harm," said Jim.

I went out to make sure; he had only pulled up several rolls of the grass and was shaking it like a rug. I began to despair what had we let ourselves in for.

SEVENTEEN

THE CAMPER VAN

For our summer holiday we decided to hire a camper van to tour Scotland. We hired a Bedford five birth van from Paul's self-drive hire in Leicester.

I did lots of cooking and freezing in readiness; large pizzas, meat pies, fruit pies cakes and pastries. I thought it would cut down the cost rather than buying and we'd have instant meals.

The children were excited when Jim arrived with the van, they couldn't wait to explore and decide where they would sleep. It was a shock to discover there was no oven, only a grill and hob and no freezer. I decided we'd still take all the things I had cooked and manage somehow.

With little storage space we could only take a few essential clothes so the children had to empty their bags which contained mostly toys and began packing again. "Sorry, son, you can't take all that stuff with you, there's only just enough room for the five of us plus the dog."

I couldn't imagine how we would all sleep or even where the dog would go.

It was a tight squeeze, but we packed everything in and were on our way. It was fun singing 'Coming round the mountains' and 'Were all going on a summer holiday,' playing I spy; something we always did to make time pass more quickly when going on holiday.

A few stops were needed to stretch ours and the dog's legs, to have a picnic and give Jim a break from driving even though they pestered him to carry on.

We travelled a long way until it was dusk and we still hadn't reached Scotland so parked in a lay by for the night. It was an eerie moonlit night, the children had to stand outside while the beds were made up. The table fitted between the two front seats to make a double bed, the girls chose this one.

Andrew chose the bunk bed above the driver's cab, "This is my secret cabin so no spying," he said.

The sofa at the end of the van pulled out to make another double bed which Jim and I would use; this only left a tiny amount of floor space for Shandy.

All we had for a toilet was a bucket but we just had to manage the best we could until we found a site with toilets and shower block.

With the light from the moon and the children's torches we got ready for bed and tried to settle down to sleep all except Shandy, he kept walking forward and reversing in the narrow space beside our bed, grunting and pushing his cold wet nose in my face.

By now I was feeling tired and irritable. "It's no good," I shouted, "I can't sleep like this, we'll just have to make more room for the dog."

Up we got again, earlier we had discovered a canvas hammock and poles to make another bed should it be needed, now was that time.

Pushing the sofa bed back gave us more floor space where Shandy immediately flopped.

Jim threaded the poles through the canvas and fitted it on the wall brackets, "You'll have to sleep up there, Jim, there's no way I could get up there."

Up he got it was only just big enough, his head hung over one end and his feet the other.

Shandy at last settled down and slept, which was more than could be said for the rest of us, especially Jim dangling from the roof.

In the morning the beds had to be packed away before we could have breakfast, it was like playing musical chairs moving around each other to get washed and dressed.

At last we were seated around the table waiting for our first holiday breakfast, Jim's favourite; bacon, eggs, sausages and mushrooms. I could see he looked happier, he had a big grin. The smell and taste were delicious and seemed to drive away all thoughts of the sleepless night.

After breakfast we all piled outside and noticed a huge American camper parked beside us. A young honeymoon couple were touring England; they stood looking astonished to see five people and one large dog emerge from such a small van. "Oh my God, where did you all come from and how did you all manage to sleep in that?" They couldn't believe their eyes.

Tour Scotland we did, finding new things to do and see, finding places to explore and creating lasting memories which the children still talk about today with real fondness.

EIGHTEEN

CAMPING HOLIDAYS

The ridge tent we had was old, a bit like the basic ones used by the army everything took place in one compartment, eating, washing, sleeping, cooking and storing all the necessary items needed for a family of five and a dog on holiday. It had looked rather primitive pitched on a campsite next to more superior models.

Many happy times had been spent in it, in the garden, at the seaside, in local fields. It had served us well while the children were small and was a cheaper way to have a holiday but thought it was time to upgrade to something more stylish.

We had seen an advertisement in the local paper for a French tent so rang to see if we could view it, the children were excited as we drove to the seller's house.

The owners had put it up for us to examine to see what state it was in and to observe them dismantling it should we decide to buy it. We couldn't believe how big it was, the children stood wide eyed taking it all in. "Wow this is like a palace we can have separate bedrooms," they shouted.

It contained sleeping compartments for six people which zipped up to keep flies and insects out, a kitchen galley, a storage area and a front porch with windows the full width.

I watched their reactions as we explored thinking how better and more luxurious holidays would be if we brought it, so we snapped it up.

We observed carefully as it was taken down in the hope we'd remember the order of things when it was time for our next holiday. They made it look very easy even though there were a lot of poles.

The owners generously included many extras, water barrels, electric hook up cable, gas cooker, and a groundsheet. It got better and better, they were as excited as we were, I could just visualise how much easier and comfortable future holidays would be with these extras, I don't know how we managed before.

Our next holiday was planned quite quickly so didn't have time for a dummy run at erecting the tent but felt sure I would remember. Packing it all in the car took a lot of room with just enough left for the children and the dog.

The camp site was near Hearn airport in Cornwall not too far from the beach. It was a beautiful sunny day with a cool breeze, perfect for our first trial with the new tent. Many campers were pitched and organised, sitting relaxing, supping refreshing drinks and barbequing food which smelt appetising.

Trying to look knowledgeable we unpacked the tent, laid the poles neatly and set about putting it together. Watching it being dismantled had appeared straight forward but now was a different matter; which pole fitted to which, some were jointed others weren't and there were so many of them.

Doing it in front of an audience was embarrassing too, the children starving and trying to be helpful said, "How much longer is it going to take we're hungry and thirsty and want to try it out."

"We are trying to be as quick as we can, just be patient a bit longer then I'll cook tea, here's a biscuit and drink for now, take the dog for a stroll to that hedge and back and here is some water for him."

Still struggling but trying to see the funny side of it, we laughed and chuckled uncomfortably with each other as we pretended to know what we were doing.

Some of the neighbours drifted over offering help and advice, "New to this game? We've been there done it and got the t-shirt, can we give you a hand mate? It's too hot to be struggling."

I was so relieved; I was worrying that Jim was finding it too much, "Thanks, we'd be very grateful. We have only just brought it and it's the first time, it appeared so easy when it was demonstrated to us." I replied rather too eagerly. "We'll have it up in no time, we've all been in similar situations," was the reply as they joined in the fun and laughter, and sure enough it was up in a flash.

The children were back almost as quickly they had been keeping an eye on the proceedings and couldn't wait to get inside.

In no time everything was unpacked and in its place, the dog had chosen his spot and the children theirs, I had chosen mine in the kitchen preparing the meal which smelt good.

We sat outside and enjoyed our meal, food tasted so much better outdoors, and our embarrassment had subsided as we reflected on what we had just achieved, how kind people were and how grand the new tent was. It felt like a palace in comparison to the old ridge tent.

This was going to be a holiday to remember.

NINETEEN

RETURNING TO NORMALITY

Jim gradually began to feel fitter and stronger so had returned to work, part time at first then increasing to full time. He was managing well. I continued full time and everything was fitting nicely together.

Mum had become more stable it seemed and had found herself a boyfriend. The relationship appeared to be serious with talk of marriage. To me and my siblings it was all rather rushed but they went ahead and she married Harry.

Harry promised all sorts of things, he was currently living in a house attached to his brother's post office and shop. It was rather bleak, cold and damp. He was the caretaker while his brother and his wife lived in a lovely detached house.

The promise of a bungalow never did materialise, Mum would cook meals and clean for them and for a while seemed content, and so we tried to feel positive.

I wanted to do something more for myself so joined Knighton Park Operatic Society, who put musicals on once a year at The

Little Theatre in Leicester. This was magical learning all the new songs, dances and script. The first show I did was South Pacific; I was a nurse in the chorus.

I was filled with excitement, tummy tied in knots, nervous and anxious not to get it wrong but full of joy when at the dress rehearsal it all came together, band, costumes, scenery, lights and sound. I couldn't wait for opening night to have an audience. From then on I was smitten.

I visited mum and Harry as often as I could to really check that she wasn't lapsing mentally as she sometimes appeared stressed. I learned that she was taking long walks especially in the evenings.

She began to show signs of instability again, she always had a strong faith and attended church but was now becoming overly religious, apparently walking across fields to pubs, taking her bible and preaching, putting herself at risk then accepting lifts home with strangers.

She was also drawing pictures of faces she said she could see in clouds, trees and shrubs. My heart sank at the thought of her probably being sectioned again, all the evidence was there.

The GP we talked with saw our concerns and managed to persuade her to go into hospital, this time she was admitted to Walsgrave Hospital at Coventry.

It felt like we were back at square one again.

The marriage didn't work out, Mum had become a skivvy and was being used and taken for granted. The accommodation or situation wasn't good for her health or well-being, so she decided to divorce Harry. She then changed her name by deed poll back to Perry, my Fathers surname. I think that even after all the abuse she'd had, deep down she still loved him.

We were fortunate to find Mum a flat in sheltered accommodation with a visiting warden where she settled down and enjoyed herself with company, activities, and she was safe. Sonia my younger sister visited to help clean the flat and bathe

Mum as she didn't go out to work and had the time, as soon as I retired, I also went and we shared the jobs.

I used to make Mum laugh, the warden often called just as I got Mum into the bath, the door was close to the bathroom door. I would open it wide and shout "Come in Vicar," to which she would shriek out loud.

It certainly felt a great relief knowing where Mum was living and that help was at hand if needed and that we didn't have to feel as worried about her.

Maybe we could get back to some sort of normality now.

TWENTY

CHILDREN

The children grew and developed. They were all happy, made friends easily, were mostly healthy, although Andrew at eleven months had a strangulated hernia and hydrocele, was admitted to hospital and strung up by his feet to enable the hernia to reduce before they could operate.

Louise had a small growth removed from a finger and they all had tonsils removed.

It was a relief to know that Jim's heart condition wouldn't be inherited.

It was at times like these that feelings were stirred that I felt when sitting on the third step of the stairs when younger, feelings I hoped I had erased but which kept popping up.

They progressed well at school all went to Cosby infant and Junior School, Louise went on to Brockington then Lutterworth, Beth and Andrew went to Thomas Estley then Countesthorpe colleges.

Louise had a part time job at a newsagent shop in Blaby; they all helped at the animal aid kennels at Huncote.

Andrew played football in the Cosby under thirteens, which Jim managed. Consequently, I always had the whole team's kit to launder.

Louise decided she was going to be a nurse. She went for interview and was accepted at Nuneaton to do a state enrolled nursing course. After spending some time working at the George Elliot hospital she came back to Leicester and became a District Nurse, after completing her RGN course.

Beth went to Chester College to do a Health and Community degree going on to work in residential care for adults with special needs. She then did a Social Work degree at Brunel University afterwards she managed a residential home for adults with special needs in Bedford.

Andrew worked in the meat industry after leaving school and went to the butchery department at Asda. He always wanted to drive lorries so did a course at Coates lorry driver training school in Leicester. He drove for Eddie Stobarts but now drives for Walkers crisps.

Louise met and married Anthony Bullous and have a daughter, Jemma, also a nurse and a son, Sam, who works with specialist lighting for yachts.

Jemma is married to Scott Billet

Beth met and married Paul Dennis, a Yorkshire man. They have a son, Joshua David and a daughter, Esther Grace.

Andrew knew his partner, Leigh Howell, from school. They have four children, three sons, Liam, Chad and Ty and daughter Chelsea Leigh. They also have four grandchildren, Bailey, Alfie, Harper-Lily and Willow Ruby.

Life continued to drift along; although we had lost our dogs to a condition which seems to affect large chested dogs where the stomach folds back on itself and large amounts of gas builds up in their system causing shock to the heart. Shandy lived until he was ten and Wilber until he was seven.

Jim was a real dog man and missed them dreadfully, so I went to the Animal Aid Kennels at Huncote and chose another to surprise him. It was almost closing time but after I'd explained our situation, that I was looking for a younger dog six months to a year, the manager fetched a little dog for me to see.

He was only six months, a cross between Corgi, Afghan and Sheepdog. He trotted up and just sat on my feet looking up at me with appealing eyes. I couldn't resist him, his name was Fraggles.

I took him straight home to Jim's delight and here he stayed for the next nineteen years. He was so gentle, never barked and sat next to Jim most of the time even lay on the bed beside him too.

He loved the grandchildren and, at Christmas, when they opened their presents he plonked himself right in the middle of the wrapping paper or jumped into an empty box to sleep. We continued to call him Fraggles.

*

Jim at times struggled and, although he was often quite tired, he still managed to work, then coming up to Christmas one year I was having a pre-Christmas dinner with nursing colleagues and got a call to say he had collapsed.

He was admitted to the Leicester Royal, his heart rhythms were out of sync and they had to shock it back into a regular beat, but his mitral valves were now incompetent, and his heart failure had worsened.

After seeing his physician he said, "Your heart won't cope with more surgery, it is a heart transplant that's required, but I don't hold out much hope. However, I'll discuss it with my surgeon colleague."

The surgeon saw us and said, "I'm prepared to give you the benefit of the doubt and will operate, you need two mechanical mitral valves so will get you booked in."

It was a relief and I couldn't thank him enough. Although

memories of our time in London with all its anxieties came flooding back, as did the feelings of sitting on the third step.

The date was set and Jim was admitted. Beth had taken time off to be with me and we were allowed to stay at the hospital overnight if we wished.

We were able to stay with him after he'd been given his pre-med, he was just about to be pushed to theatre when the doctor came and said, "We have to cancel the op as your blood result has just come back and it shows that your thyroid is underactive it would be dangerous to proceed."

We couldn't believe it but home we went, mentally exhausted – and Jim frustrated but not showing any anger – and waited for another date.

The operation eventually went ahead, and he made a good but slow recovery. He had been working for the NHS at this time in the Mental Health Unit as a maintenance joiner.

As he had collapsed at work they were now assessing his capabilities to work. They refused to allow him to drive, use electrical equipment or climb ladders health and safety were very strict which meant it was almost impossible to be employed so after many meetings he took early retirement.

This did very little for his morale and at times he felt quite low. He began cooking meals again, taking the dog for walks and generally trying to be useful.

In December 1999 I decided to take early retirement to be more available and for us to do more together.

I had a great send off from work; a party, a watch and pictures from staff and a cake designed by the Nursing Director. It was lovely seeing so many nursing colleagues from the Trust present, although I did have some misgivings that I would miss the company.

One of the first things we decided to do was to go on a cruise to Norway with Eve and Arthur, my sister-in-law and her husband, so we immediately booked.

TWENTY ONE

THE CRUISE TO NORWAY

Excitedly we packed and set off for our holiday and, even though Jim didn't like dressing up, he had brought a second-hand evening suit in readiness for the Captains dinner. I packed my long evening dress.

We picked the ship up at Harwich and found our cabin, it was quite small but with twin beds, a small shower, a wardrobe and dressing table I felt we would manage, after all I told myself the cabin would only be used for sleeping in.

Literature about the ship and itineraries about excursions were in our cabin with information about meals, activities and entertainment. It informed us we would have a daily bulletin as to where we were on our journey and any changes that might take place.

We chose three excursions; one included a coach trip up into the mountains to a Sami village to see the reindeer and the people who lived in Tepees, which was a mock up for tourists.

It was very relaxing on board several restaurants, lounges, cinema, a theatre with entertainment of singers, dancers and comedians. There were also midnight themed meals with carved shaped fruit and vegetables if one could eat any more.

During the day there were deck quoits and skittles, on the lower decks there was ballroom dancing, card tables, and sessions were held on how to turn table napkins into animals or flowers and carving melons into decorative items.

There was plenty to do in between drinking tea, coffee and cakes or visiting the different bars, not that we drank very much alcohol.

I had taken our video camera and tried to capture as much as I could. Up on the top deck one day people were gathered staring up into the mountains. Apparently a golden eagle had been spotted. It was so high up it was difficult to tell but I aimed the camera and pressed the button and hoped. When I checked later all I could see was mountain tops and sky.

Being February, it was pretty cold on deck, but the scenery and glaciers were spectacular, and I did capture some on the video.

On the first Tuesday four days into our trip Jim began to feel unwell, shivering and feeling clammy he took some paracetamol and felt a bit better. It was the Captains dinner that night, "Come on, Jim, we can't miss this special event. Put your suit on we don't have to stay all evening."

He did, reluctantly. We had photographs taken with the Captain, then as soon as the meal was over, he couldn't wait to get his suit off and went back to the cabin to put something more comfortable on.

He later started to look slightly jaundiced and had night time rigors with profuse sweating.

I couldn't believe what was happening again, and so far from home on a ship too. My mind was jumping to all sorts of conclusions; was it his heart, another bout of bacterial endocarditis or a bug he'd picked up on the ship?

I was sick with worry especially when he began to hallucinate. I had to ask for more towels to absorb the perspiration. I took him to the ships doctor and told him about his history and the current symptoms.

The doctor took a series of blood tests to grow for culture to see if he had got endocarditis. He advised to continue paracetamol, push fluids and try to get his temperature down and to rest.

For three days his condition seemed to worsen. He couldn't eat and lost interest. The doctor took daily bloods to see if there were any changes, I was almost beside myself as Jim wasn't improving.

I kept fetching iced drinks to try to tempt him and small meals which the crew in the restaurants prepared for me to take back to the cabin. I went for meals to the restaurants, but Jim couldn't be persuaded. I also spent some time taking a walk on deck especially when we had docked and almost everyone had left the ship to go on an excursion. I recorded the vista from the deck, it was like a ghost ship.

We continued sailing and on the Friday the ship was due to dock at Trondheim as this was one of the excursions. After the doctor had seen Jim he said, "I've arranged for you to go into hospital here, you need an intense course of intravenous antibiotics and we only carry so much on board. I can't determine what is going on, but you have a severe infection of some sort."

I felt a sense of relief to some degree but terrified in another. I felt all alone again, in a foreign country too glad to be getting off the ship and to get a diagnosis of what was happening to Jim.

The doctor said, "I've faxed all the details ahead to the cardiologist, so they are aware of what's been happening, and a taxi is coming to collect you both, you'll be in good hands."

Before we had got back to the cabin the medical invoices had been pushed under the door and the ship's stewards arrived shortly after for us to settle the bill for the doctor and for things we had spent on the ship like drinks etc. I settled up immediately.

Jim lay exhausted on the bed while I hurriedly packed the two cases. I couldn't find his wallet so searched the cases a second time and, to my relief, eventually found it in his dinner jacket.

In no time it seemed the taxi arrived, we said a tearful goodbye to Eve and Arthur and, with the help of porters, we slowly eased our way down the gang plank and were soon at the hospital.

At the hospital we were taken into an admission ward where a doctor quickly appeared. I dreaded it, not being able to speak Norwegian, but needn't have worried as he spoke perfect English.

Jim was always a man of few words and preferred me to talk to professionals about anything medical so I carried on explaining all about his heart operation in London, that he had had the Ross procedure and the subsequent things that had occurred plus the symptoms while on the ship.

The doctor was smiling as I was explaining, then said, "I trained in London with Donald Ross so know all about your procedure, it is one that is used worldwide and is very successful."

I almost cried with relief it was such a comfort to learn this and I felt Jim was in safe hands.

He proceeded to examine Jim thoroughly then said, "I don't think this is your heart I think it is your gall bladder causing all your problems. We'll send you for an immediate ultrasound take bloods and see."

He was whisked away and I waited in a side ward where Jim would go after his tests. The hospital took precautions that we weren't carriers of MRSA so until the results came back I had to mask and gown and Jim was in isolation.

"The results show that you have a very highly inflamed gall bladder. The stones have become like sludge it's a bit like an abscess waiting to burst so we will admit you and give you strong intra-venous antibiotics to reduce the infection, we can't remove it, and it is too dangerous."

I couldn't thank him enough; all the staff were attentive and could speak very good English and we weren't carriers of MRSA, so Jim was put into a main ward.

I started to wonder where I could stay but they gave me a room within the hospital grounds in accommodation kept for relatives. This too was such a relief.

All I had to do now was to notify the family, the hospital even gave me a line I could use to contact them daily or they could contact me by arranging time. I could also get in touch with mine and Jim's insurance.

I rang home to let them all know what was happening and gave them the contact telephone number. Louise wasn't in, so I spoke to Anthony, her husband.

"Hi Anthony, I'm just ringing to let you know that we have had to get off the ship as Jim is ill. He's been taken into hospital in Trondheim. Could you let Louise know and she can let the others know please."

He was taken back a little and I explained what had been happening, but thought I had assured him that things were under control.

Not long later Louise rang, "What's happening, is Dad alright? We're going to fly out. Bill wants to fly out too, we're all worried." Bill was one of our neighbours who we had had holidays with. "Where are you staying and how are you managing."

I tried to put her mind at rest explaining again what the consultant had said but she took some convincing.

Shortly after a call came in from Beth, "I can't believe you two, you're miles away from home again and stuck in hospital, how did you manage that? I'm going to come straight out."

Again, I tried to impress that Jim was having the right treatment, that it wasn't his heart but his gall bladder which was very infected and that we were ok and being well looked after.

A further call came from Andrew. "Are you alright, Mum?

How's Dad? Take care of yourselves." He had been filled in by Beth and Louise so was fully in the picture.

They rang every day, which was a real comfort. The room that I stayed in was very basic but clean and comfortable; it was cleaned daily by a well-built young Norwegian boy. He must have been in his late twenties. One day he had stuck a note on the wash basin. "To the English woman, will you be my friend, and talk with me as I want to learn English and one day come to England. "and signed Henryk,

He was very helpful, showed me where the bank in the hospital was, where the local shop was so that I could buy food. I hadn't enough Norwegian currency one day, so he lent me some until I'd got some more cash.

One day he strolled with me along by the river and was really keen to learn.

Each day I went walking into Trondheim to the cathedral where I went inside and spent a lot of time in its sanctuary. If the weather was fine the square by the cathedral was a pleasant place to sit and people watch or drink coffee from the little coffee stall.

I found a McDonalds and had burger and chips, cheap but cheerful. It made me think of the children and how they always loved this place.

The hospital invited me to go in to see Jim at any time, especially lunch time. Often they served me a meal with him, although more often than not it was meat balls and boiled potatoes, but beggars can't be choosers.

Jim progressed really well. He had drips into both arms where strong antibiotics were fed into his veins and gradually his fever subsided, although the surgeon said it was too dangerous to remove the gall bladder as it was like an abscess. He would have to go to hospital as soon as he came home to have it removed.

Towards the end of his stay I was allowed to take Jim out in a wheelchair so was able to show him some of the sights I had explored.

I kept a daily log of all that was happening to Jim, all the phone calls I was making, all the information I was receiving for the insurances both mine and Jim's. The insurance companies were very good, wanting to keep up to date with his progress and as soon as we had a discharge date they gave us travel instructions.

The day arrived, staff had been wonderful. It felt quite emotional saying our goodbyes we couldn't thank them enough. Jim was tearful with relief.

I'd rung the children the night before they were so excited.

A taxi was laid on to take us from the hospital to the airport in Trondheim where we caught a flight to Oslo.

The plane had been held up especially for us, a porter was waiting with a wheelchair for Jim, but I had to belt alongside them to keep up. I have never been so breathless, no way was I going to let this plane go without us. Then we were on our flight to Heathrow.

At Heathrow the Red Cross had arranged for a taxi to take us home to Leicester. Seeing our names on a placard at the exit was wonderful – I knew we were almost home

"Let me know if you want to stop at any time on the way back, just shout"

"No thanks we'll just keep going," said Jim.

We left London at around eleven pm so knew it would be late getting home, when we pulled up the house lights were on decorations were up and pictures from the grandchildren were stuck on the walls. Louise and Beth stood grinning from ear to ear, pouncing on us to give us a hug

In my relief I nearly forgot to thank the driver but did offer him a drink.

It felt so good to be home.

We quickly re-established ourselves into a routine; neighbours eager to chat about our dilemma called regularly, the children made extra visits to make sure we were behaving.

After visiting the GP, Jim was referred very quickly to the hospital and he didn't have to wait too long before he was called to have his gall bladder removed.

Hospital visits and admissions had become a way of life for us so we just took it all in our stride, Jim still uncomplaining.

Our family continued to grow with the arrival of our beautiful grandchildren. I gave what support I could in terms of child-minding, which enabled their mums and dads to go out to work, it was necessary for them to be able to have mortgages, run their cars, support and provide for their own families.

They frequently came for sleepovers and family meals, something I thoroughly enjoyed. We took them out for day trips and to fun parks – it enabled me to keep young at heart and Jim came along for the ride.

It was special when all the cousins were together; they had such fun and have remained friends since.

We purchased a little two berth touring caravan and brought an awning which slept four or more so that we could take the children with us.

We stayed at local sites, Bosworth Water Park or Ullesthorpe garden centre who had a field for caravans next door to the garden centre.

We were here with four of the grandchildren and having a whale of a time when Jim began to slur his speech. He appeared to lose some sensation and co-ordination, I called for an ambulance as I realised he was having a stroke. They arrived almost immediately as they had been parked at Lutterworth just a mile away and whipped him off to hospital. I said, "I'll follow you as soon as I've sorted the children out."

Staff from the garden centre saw the ambulance arrive and dashed over to help, I called Anthony, my son-in law, who had his own business at home in Broughton Astley "Hi Anthony, guess what it's me again. Jim's having a stroke. They've taken him to hospital, is Jemma around or could you come and fetch the children."

Fortunately Jemma was at home so they took the kids and sorted them out, much to their disappointment that their fun had been cut short.

I dashed to the Leicester Royal infirmary and caught up with Jim in A and E from where he was admitted to a ward. The stroke had affected his left side his speech and swallowing.

He recovered his speech and swallowing and after some rehabilitation was discharged home but with a struggle.

We had to think about home adaptations, some aids were provided by the Red Cross, a walking frame, toilet seat raiser, hand rails were fixed by the door. I enquired what financial help was available towards having a shower installed or a wet room and for a stair lift as Jim was really struggling.

After a financial assessment we were told that we were just borderline so didn't qualify, so did it ourselves. Five thousand pounds for a walk in shower and for the bath to be removed, five thousand pounds for a downstairs toilet and five thousand pounds for a stair lift.

Social Services said. "If you purchase the stair lift we will service it for you annually but then it becomes our property." I asked. "What happens when something happens to Jim, do I keep it for my use?" "No, it will be removed." I couldn't believe what I was hearing.

Jim continued making slow progress at home but was determined, managing to get around with his frame which he hated using, I pushed the wheelchair when we went out, and tried to think of places to take him or things to do to break the monotony of being stuck indoors.

On days we had hospital appointments we followed it up with a meal at a nearby pub, we visited garden centres or went to the cinema. I sometimes had to bully him a bit to make the effort to go out but most of the time he said he had enjoyed it.

He resented the fact that I had to push the chair, he'd been aware that my arthritis was getting worse and I was having pain in my right hip and he felt he was a burden.

I said, "Let's go and get a mobility scooter so you can be more independent." So off we went to choose one that would take apart to go in the car.

He drove it up and down the street outside the warehouse and was smitten. I was shown how to dismantle it and put it together again and we were away.

We were now finding it a bit easier to visit parks and gardens where he enjoyed the freedom the scooter allowed, he raced along leaving me puffing and running up in the rear.

We still visited garden centres where he loved hiding from me, when he could see me coming he'd change direction and hide down another aisle, and I spent ages trying to find him.

We did manage to go on a couple of coach holidays or day trips.

I was now getting severe pain in my hip and, after being threatened by the family to go to the doctors, I had to have a hip replacement. Another episode of anxiety and worry – how would Jim manage, Louise was working full time, Andrew was lorry driving and was away a lot, Beth was living in Bedford. It felt impossible, but I knew the pain was too much to ignore.

After being reassured that the family would pull together the operation went ahead, fortunately I was only in for a week and given strict instructions not to do anything stupid and was soon back managing the housework. The hardest part was not being able to drive for six weeks but then there was no holding me back.

Jim was managing much better although I was still helping him shower. We continued to live a good life, but then Mum began to deteriorate. She was admitted to hospital and diagnosed with a type of Leukaemia. While an inpatient she picked up a norovirus infection and was quite ill.

Now being frail and requiring rehabilitation the hospital

suggested she went into residential care, they recommended a home in Nuneaton who offered this so Mum was transferred.

The idea of mum in a home appalled all of us, her children, and I felt especially guilty, being a nurse, that I wasn't caring for her. She was very unhappy, not receiving any rehab, in a room on her own, not being taken to the lounge to see others and was isolated.

Sonia my sister and I visited daily and could see the neglect and deterioration.

After discussions with my other siblings who had visited when they could as they lived further away we decided that Mum would come to stay with me,

Together we organised our spare bedroom fetched her reclining chair to enable her to sit out and arranged a private ambulance to transfer her.

Pearl and Rosemary my sisters were both nurses as was Louise my daughter and granddaughter Jemma and niece Emma, they agreed to share the care when they could and we applied to register Mum with a local GP and request nursing care.

I provided her meals helped feed her and gave care when necessary, other nieces visited and helped with ironing and anything else they could.

By now she was terminally ill but it was a comfort to know she was with us and being well cared for and all the family visited her.

One morning Jim came down on the stair lift and didn't seem to be engaging. When he began to talk his speech was affected and his words were not making sense.

"Not again," I almost screamed to myself, and sure enough he was in the process of having another stroke, he was admitted to the stroke unit at Leicester City General. Fortunately, family members were at my house so organised a rota to care for Mum and I followed the ambulance.

Mum's condition was deteriorating rapidly. I felt very torn to be with Jim or to stay with Mum as I could see she was in final stages, so went dutifully with Jim.

I was allowed to ring home to see how things were.

It was a long time waiting for Jim to be seen by the doctors and at about ten pm Beth and my niece, Laura, came to the hospital to see how we were. It was shortly after this that Mum died.

Jim was kept in for a few days and then allowed home. On the day I went to collect him with Louise we had called in at a Waitrose store in Blaby to get a few provisions and, on the way out on the mini roundabout, someone ran their car into me. I had right of way and they weren't looking. I threw my arms up in despair and shouted, "What else can go wrong I can't believe it I'm doomed." Louise got out and confronted the driver, "What were you thinking? Mum's just lost her mum; her husband's had a stroke and now this."

I calmed down and found the necessary paper work, exchanged insurance details and checked the car, fortunately it wasn't too badly damaged and was still drivable.

We proceeded to collect Jim who was by now pacing the corridor with his frame looking for us wondering why we were late. After an explanation he was ok and got home in one piece.

How I longed for normality and life without incidents.

Mum's funeral was held in the tiny chapel in the grounds of Caldecote Hall. Mum had worshipped here and Caldecote was where she had rebuilt her life and had been very happy.

The last time we had all been here together as a family was at Wendy, my youngest sister's, wedding.

The chapel was packed with family, friends and neighbours with people standing at the back too, her son, sons-in-law and grandsons carried the coffin and did her proud. She would have been delighted.

Afterwards, we went for a meal to a nearby restaurant. All of my siblings and their respective partners were gathered. It was a joyful occasion with lots of fun and laughter, so much that we vowed we should get together more often and not wait for an event to occur to arrange it.

We kept to our word, and the following year we hired an old farmhouse in Lancashire where twelve of us stayed. There were log fires in the two big lounges. The farm was named Batty farm and couldn't have been more appropriate with us mad lot staying there.

We held a murder mystery night where everyone dressed up and got into character. This caused great hilarity; everyone had made a real effort to look their part.

A day was spent preparing food. It was a banquet and was eaten at specific points during the play.

A large case full of photographs belonging to Mum which had ended up at my house was opened up, we spread them all over the table and spent a day pouring over them reminiscing over who was who, when they were taken, how old we were and who should claim which. We didn't fall out over them as we'd agreed to get copies done if needed.

It was a good job there were no neighbouring houses as we screamed with laughter at some of them and had stomach cramps as a result.

I don't think any of us had laughed as much in a long time; it sure was therapeutic and so worthwhile.

TWENTY TWO

MUSICAL THEATRE

Since 1978 I had pursued my love of acting and passion for musical theatre, belonging to two operatic societies gave me this opportunity, and filled a year nicely without any overlapping.

Knighton Park Amateur Operatic Society (KPAOS) rehearsed from June until November when the show was performed at The Little Theatre in Dover Street Leicester.

Leicester Amateur Operatic Society (LAOS) rehearsed from December until June. This society had been in existence since 1890 and had used different venues to perform their shows.

I was overjoyed to receive a phone call one day from Lilian Dunkley, the director and producer of the 'Amateurs' as they were always referred to. She was held in high esteem and awe by the members and was known to be a strict disciplinarian.

I couldn't believe that I, a mere mortal, could get a call of this nature inviting me to join them for their next production of *Hello Dolly* to play the part of Ernestina, it was being put on at the Haymarket Leicester, I was dumbstruck, star struck and very flattered.

She did remind me that I would need to go to her house to formally audition so that she could hear me sing. Thankfully after being so hyped up I was successful.

Treading the boards at this beautiful theatre was exhilarating; we performed here until its initial closure in 2003. Since then performances have taken place at The Little Theatre, De Montfort Hall and in 2009 we moved to the newly built theatre Curve where we presented a production of The Full Monty to a capacity audience.

The 'Amateurs' have now returned to the Haymarket Theatre once again, following its refurbishment in 2018.

Shows which I have performed in are:

For the Leicester Amateurs:
- Hello Dolly (Ernestina) 1983
- Guys and Dolls (General Cartwright) 1984
- No No Nanette 1986
- My Fair Lady 1987
- Annie (Cook) 1988
- Kiss Me Kate 1989
- South Pacific (nurse) 1991
- Gentlemen Prefer Blondes (Chorus) 1992
- Anything Goes (Evangeline Harcourt) 1993
- 42nd Street Chorus (1994
- Barnum 1995 *De Montfort Hall*
- Fiddler on The Roof 1996
- Me and My Girl (Lady Battersby) 1997
- Crazy for You 1998 (Chorus)
- My Fair Lady 1999
- State Fair 2001
- Jolson 2002

- Jesus Christ Superstar 2003
- The Full Monty 2009 *Curve Theatre*
- Jesus Christ Superstar 2014 *Curve Theatre*
- Sister Act (Sister Mary Theresa) 2015
- 9 to 5 2016 *Curve Studio*
- Parade 2017 *Curve Studio*
- Chitty Chitty Bang Bang 2018 *Haymarket Theatre.*

For Knighton Park Operatic Society at the Little Theatre:
- South Pacific 1978 *Mary Linwood School*
- Calamity Jane 1979
- Pyjama Game (Mabel) 1980
- Guys and Dolls (General Cartwright) 1981
- Oliver (Mrs Bumble) 1982
- Half a Sixpence (Lady Botting) 1984
- South Pacific 1985
- Kiss Me Kate 1986
- Carousel 1987
- Hello Dolly (Ernestina) 1988
- Charlie Girl 1989
- Fiddler On The Roof 1990
- Calamity Jane 1991
- Irene (Mrs O'Dare) 1992
- Oklahoma (Aunt Eller) 1994
- Music Man 1995
- South Pacific (Bloody Mary) 1997
- Oliver (Mrs Bumble) 1998
- Half A Sixpence (Lady Walsingham) 1999
- Annie (Cook) 2000
- Me and My Girl (Lady Beakman) 2002
- Oliver (Mrs Bedwin) 2007
- Copacabana 2009
- Annie (Cook) 2013

- Oh What A Lovely War 2014
- Hairspray (Prison Officer) 2015
- Summer Holiday (Doris) 2016
- Dirty Rotten Scoundrels 2017
- Spamalot 2018

In addition to these I performed in a professional production of Oliver at The De Montfort Hall when Denise Nolan played Nancy and Tony Altman played Bill Sykes, I played Widow Corney.

Being in all of these shows has been a great leveller in my life, it has provided me with great friendships, stimulation, a purpose, something to strive to and challenge me with. It often gave me a chance to escape from reality; characters to hide behind, a sense of joy and fulfilment, an opportunity to be creative and I hope it may long continue.

TWENTY THREE

KISSOGRAMME

I received a telephone call from an acting and model agent inviting me to join her agency. She had been looking for someone with a good sense of humour who liked comedy and a client on her books had mentioned my name.

It was apparently someone who had been in shows with me who knew I could be funny when necessary. I enquired further what the job might entail and discovered it was to become a Kissagramme Girl.

I wasn't too sure what to think, what situations I might find myself in. After all I had a respectable job and what would happen if it was revealed to my employers what I got up to in my spare time, not that I would have done anything indiscreet.

I reassured myself that it was just an extension of my acting and so, after giving it some thought and chatting to the family, I accepted and had a meeting with the agent. I asked, "What am I expected to do, what costumes will I wear and where will the venues be?"

She replied. "You'll be booked as a Roly Poly Kissagramme. You can use your imagination and respond in any way you want or however comfortable you feel. I suggest you could be a nurse or a fairy or a maid."

I was provided with a large piece of pink netting out of which I made a ballet skirt, I already had a pair of pink ballet tights and a black leotard and ballet slippers. I made a suitable crown and decided that was enough, I'd give wings a miss.

The first booking was at a large posh manor house near Rugby, it was a birthday party for a member of a Rugby club.

Beth insisted on coming with me, to ensure my safety I think.

I arrived in costume at the appointed time to find a hall full of burly Rugby players who shrieked with laughter and escorted me to the stage where the celebrity stood. They lifted me in the air and passed me along the row where I ended up in a wrestling hug to much hilarity.

Fortunately my costume didn't come adrift or tear as the event was quite physical.

I felt it had been a successful interlude even though Beth thought I might have got injured.

The second booking was a real surprise as Sue Townsend of "the Diary of Adrian Mole" fame had booked me for her manager's birthday. They were filming the series and were on location in Leicester where they had a caravan.

Sue met me and invited me into the van to get changed. I decided again to wear my ballet outfit, it covered a lot of me and I felt secure. She then summoned her manager who came inside, I immediately pounced and gave him a hug swinging him round; fortunately he was quite small built and lightweight so managed to manhandle him easily.

He was thrilled with her surprise.

So far so good, I thought to myself, although I still had niggling doubts that it wasn't the 'done' thing or the proper image for a nurse.

I had a request to attend a restaurant for a man's birthday party to surprise him with his cake, I made a maid's outfit for this with thick black tights, short black skirt, white blouse and apron and a little cap, all very decent.

I hid under the table and when they were seated pushed my way out through the birthday boy's legs and sat on his knee. It was a tricky manoeuvre as there wasn't much space to get out. I then fetched the cake on a trolley and did the honours.

This event felt uncomfortable in front of other diners and I wasn't too sure if the recipients had been completely satisfied so decided I would hang up my ballet shoes and stick to musical theatre.

TWENTY FOUR

JIM'S DEPARTING

Jim continued to have recurring small strokes, each one more debilitating, making him lose more of his independence and increasing his frustrations.

He never expressed anger, just sank into a state of withdrawal and was even quieter than before. He seldom spoke about what his feelings were even though I tried to wheedle them out of him, I occasionally got a chuckle, but they were short lived.

One day I was out watering the front garden and could see him through the window. I was messing with the hose and gesturing that I would spray him and aimed it at the window which did make him laugh.

While packing the hose away I heard a bang and discovered he'd fallen and hurt his leg. Paramedics were called and we got him up to see if he could stand, he had difficulty weight bearing but still didn't complain of pain but went to hospital for an X-ray.

The fall occurred at six pm the ambulance arrived at midnight.

We were queuing in corridors on a trolley until almost two am. After X-ray and history taking he was transferred to an orthopaedic ward as he had sustained a fractured hip and would require surgery.

Surgery took place later the next day where some complications had arisen due to the anaesthetic, but he was returned to the orthopaedic ward.

Due to Jim's complex medical history it was difficult to deal with him in orthopaedics so he was transferred to a side ward on a medical unit.

After caring for Jim so long at home no way was I going to leave him at hospital and not be by his side so I made the decision that I would stay as long as necessary day or night.

The staff didn't object or say that I couldn't, I offered to help with his care, Louise, Jemma, Andrew and family members came and spent what time they could and helped with the care too.

Jim had made it clear to our own GP and to the hospital that he didn't want to be resuscitated, at first Jim was conscious and his needs were met, he was able to drink a little and respond but gradually his organs began to fail and drifted into unconsciousness.

He had a syringe driver which controlled his pain, oxygen and a drip were in place, the care given was exceptional as was the support given to us all, when I stayed at night I was offered sandwiches, drinks a blanket and a chair to put my feet up on.

It had always been Jim's desire to die at home and I was sad that this situation had arisen to prevent that happening.

A young staff nurse was chatting to me she said. "I've been reading Jim's notes and see that it is Jim's wish to spend his final days at home, would you like that to happen because it can be arranged. We can request Hospice at home care where we get equipment put in place and nurses to visit to support you."

I said, "How long would it take, and would Jim be strong enough, I would like to fulfil his last wishes."

She said it could be arranged in two days, so I agreed. Beth was at home and she would ring the hospital the minute the hospital bed arrived and then the ward would get an ambulance booked to bring Jim home.

Jemma who was trained in travelling with unconscious patients had volunteered to travel home with Jim.

All the cogs were in place and, early on the Monday morning, Jim came home, although he struggled a bit on the way.

We got him settled and as comfortable as possible, the whole family were present and popped in to see Jim. I was spending a quiet moment by his side. It was all very peaceful, and he let out one big sigh and passed. The Hospice nurse arrived just as it all happened.

It was as if Jim had said, "I'm home now I can let go."

The funeral was a family affair, a real celebration of a much-loved husband, father, brother and friend. It was attended by many who knew Jim and had fond memories of him.

Beth had put together a DVD of his photographs. Some were quite comical and others more serious. This was shown during the service. All of the children spoke of their memories and what he had meant to them, Jemma and Chelsea both read a poem. Memories were shared by many.

TWENTY FIVE

THE EMPTY NEST

Life moves on, progresses and changes, bringing with it trials and tribulations. My nest feels really empty. The children have moved on, living their own lives with their offspring.

I reflect on how my role has changed from daughter to sibling to career girl to wife, mother, grandmother and now a widow. Once again single, unattached: how strange and frightening it feels.

I try to hang on to every moment to relive memories of love, joy, and happiness but sadness seeps through blocking thoughts of what has been.

Jim's character is everywhere – his craftsmanship a constant reminder of his skills, as if his presence was still here in the very fabric of the rooms.

It's difficult to grasp that the things we shared, decisions we made together. I now have to undertake alone, yet decisions have to be made to enable me to move on.

There are so many things to sort, clothes, tools, books by

the score, an avid reader, one would think he had contemplated starting a book shop.

I start a pile of each, hesitate, then quickly put some back in the cupboards. Maybe the children would like to choose something as a reminder of their dad, perhaps then I wouldn't feel so guilty.

Plucking up courage I take things to the charity shops and hope and pray that I don't see them displayed or anyone wearing them, consoling myself that others might benefit from my misfortune.

I really must declutter, starting with the attic. This, I know, will be a mammoth task; this dumping ground for everything no longer used but too good to throw away.

I kept telling the children, "If you don't take your things now you'll have it all to do when we pop our clogs."

They just laughed and said, "Don't be daft, you and Dad aren't going anywhere." So I heave myself up the ladder into the attic, groping for the light switch. What is revealed is not so much of an Aladdin's cave but more a scene from hoarders.

Jim must have foreseen this, putting in a good, strong floor to hold the amount of stuff stashed away.

I clamber over old cases looking inside; baby clothes, special – some lovingly hand knitted by relatives, why had I kept these? With three children I had had no intention of having more. Well I suppose these could go for a start.

In the corner I spot my old Dansette record player which was long made redundant and replaced with more modern technology; this used to give us hours of pleasure.

Beside it collecting dust a box of old vinyl records. Pausing, I search through them. I'm immediately transported back Frank Sinatra, Nat King Cole, Benny Goodman and Mario Lanza.

Our favourite was Johnny Mathis, his song *My Love for You*. I get goose bumps as I remember sitting in the back seat of the car kissing goodnight and hearing it on the radio when we were courting, and one I had played at Jim's funeral.

I see the tent and a ton of camping gadgets, and recall what fun these holidays were, we started off simply with just a tent and a few simple necessities and ended up taking a trailer full of equipment, so much that it was like moving house.

In another box I find a pair of black and white stiletto shoes I wore in my heyday, I was more of a classy dresser then and could strut my stuff, we'd dance intimately until the early hours; how styles have changed.

There are boxes of Christmas decorations collected over the years. Jim always loved Christmas and got so much joy watching the children unwrap their presents even though he did very little of the preparations, except for taking the children to Lewis's department store on Christmas Eve to see Santa, to help him choose my present and to purchase a large cooked ham.

How long I've spent up here I don't know, I've been completely lost in my thoughts and have made very little impression having really just shuffled things about.

A bell suddenly pierces the silence jolting me back to the present, there's someone at the door. Oh well the decluttering will have to wait a bit longer, as I lower myself down and close the door on the past.

TWENTY SIX

MOVING ON

The house now seems large and empty, everywhere is quiet and still, I have the television or the radio on constantly to provide background noise even though I don't really absorb what's playing or being shown.

The silence is unbearable, especially at weekends. I make a decision that life was mine for the making, for the sake of our children I have to snap out of this apathy and self–pity and try to move on.

For a period of time my life had been on hold while caring for Jim. It was now time to pick up the threads and re–visit old friends, re-join the operatic societies and get more involved in church.

At church I joined the worship group; singing, whether at church or in productions was very therapeutic. Also I had made many friends there and they had given me strength and support during Jim's final days and at the funeral.

I met my neighbour, Ivor, and chatted about old times with Croft Players and about hobbies. He told me about a creative writing group he belonged to. this was something I had wanted to do when I retired, but due to Jim's health it hadn't been possible. I asked, "Would there be any possibility that I could join?"

Ivor said, "I'm sure it would be fine come with me next week."

Tentatively, I went along. it had been a long time since I had engaged my brain in anything creative; my grammar left a lot to be desired. They were a very experienced group –some had published books, produced articles for magazines and had entered and been successful in competitions.

I needn't have worried, even though they were all talented they made me welcome.

I was now able to be in two shows a year and was delighted to be cast in Sister Act and be on the main stage at Curve Theatre. My excitement bubbled over, it was such a fun show to be in and gave me goose bumps.

In February 2017 I was invited to participate in a short film called "Betty". It was written by Jordan Hanford, a friend from the Operatic Society who had branched out into script writing for short films.

The theme was dementia, a subject which he had personally witnessed in his own family, as his grandma had suffered from it. He wanted to show the devastating effects this condition had on his family members.

The film captures a chance conversation of two people on a park bench where it becomes evident that Betty has dementia.

I was thrilled to be asked and partnered John Ghent, who is a well-known actor and director at the Little Theatre in Leicester. John played Eric, Betty's husband.

The filming took place on a cold wet Sunday morning at a park in Scraptoft. It was professionally done with a film crew, cameras lights and sound, a canopy had been erected over the bench to keep the rain off and after thirteen takes it was completed in one day.

There were only a few interruptions, one from a jogger who shouted "What you doing then?" and another from a dog who sniffed around the food and drinks station.

Natural sound effects were from a flock of birds which flew over and some children who were playing football in the background.

"Betty" was entered into the short film festival, was short listed and shown on the big screen at Phoenix Arts in Leicester. It felt very strange seeing myself on a big screen, but it was satisfying to see the final product.

Since releasing it for public viewing it has received over five hundred hits and had some excellent reviews. I have been very fortunate to find how many friends I have and what a wonderful family I have too, urging me on, encouraging me and supporting me on my new journey. It's thanks to them that I have been enabled to move on.

I have overcome many things in my life, have good memories and sad and painful ones, the important thing now is living in the present.

I won't let the difficulties of the past drag me down or define me, I refuse to dwell on what has been, and thoughts of the future don't frighten me.

The experiences of childhood and images of the third step of the stairs have long faded and no longer interrupt my mind; in fact, I think they have shaped me and made me stronger.

I consider myself lucky, surrounded by love, family and friendships, I haven't lost my sense of humour I retain my independence and my faith strengthens me.

I am a survivor.

ACKNOWLEDGEMENTS

Grateful thanks go to Liz Ringrose and the Cosby writers, a creative writing group I joined following the death of Jim. This gave me something to focus on.

Your guidance support and critiquing was valuable and spurred me on.

To Kat Etoe for proof reading.

To my daughter Beth for assistance with editing and helping me to make sense of my story.

To my nephew Simon Woolerton BA FHEA for your lovely front cover design, you have captured the mood of how it felt sitting on the third step of the stairs.

To my wonderful children for your love and help in providing the memories which fill this book.

To all the other characters and situations included in my life which have made this memoir possible.

Finally grateful thanks to the publishing team at Matador for your support encouragement and professionalism in producing my book.

Thank you